LOON IN MY BATHTUB

Loon
in
My
Bathtub

RONALD ROOD

THE NEW ENGLAND PRESS
Shelburne, Vermont

ACKNOWLEDGMENTS

There are many who helped in the preparation of this book. There's the kind permission to quote from her late husband's book (*Our Animal Neighbors* by Alan Devoe—McGraw-Hill, 1953), given to me by Mary Berry Gwinn. There's the inspiration given me as a child by Thornton W. Burgess and nurtured as a youth by Mrs. Ruby North, my grammar-school teacher. There's the understanding, always, of Peg and the children, who gave up many woodland hikes and fishing trips while I sat inside and wrote what fun it was to be outside.

There's also the forbearance of the oil man, the insurance man and a few other creditors while this was being written. And my thanks go, too, to Patty Hier, that most valued of a writer's accomplices—a wonderful manuscript typist.

Most of all, my gratitude to the countless others who have helped this book come into being—the wild creatures which share our world. They have enriched the lives of millions, but there are few to tell their story. I am certainly one of the former. I hope, also, to be one of the latter. RONALD ROOD

ISBN 0-933050-28-3
Library of Congress Catalog Card Number: 85-61031
Printed in the United States of America

Originally published by The Stephen Greene Press
[ISBN 0-8289-0228-3]

For additional copies, write to:
The New England Press
P. O. Box 575
Shelburne, Vermont 05482

This book is dedicated to the memory of my cousin, Warren Catlin Reynolds, who, although he appears nowhere else on these pages, shared many a canoe ride and fishing trip with me before his life was taken from him on a European battlefield.

So teach us to number our days,
that we may apply our hearts unto wisdom.

PSALM 90:12

CONTENTS

1. BLAME MR. BURGESS 1

2. WHAT ARE LITTLE BOYS MADE OF? 11

3. FORGOTTEN SWAMP 19

4. ONE ACRE OF RACCOONS 31

5. CHASING GHOSTS 42

6. DROWSY 'CHUCKS, SLEEPY MONKEYS,
    AND LADY MACBETH 61

7. HOW DO YOU BATHE A LOON? 82

8. ACROSS THE BRIDGE 91

9. BREADLINE 101

10. MECHANICAL MICE 111

11. "MAN IS A MAMMA" 131

12. BUSMAN'S HOLIDAY 139

13. FULL CIRCLE 150

14. WITH A FEW SIMPLE THINGS . . . 164

INDEX 173

LOON IN MY BATHTUB

CHAPTER ONE

Blame Mr. Burgess

"PEG, we just got a new shipment of lettuce. Do you want some outside leaves for your porcupine?"

"Thanks, but we don't have him at home any more."

"Then how about your muskrat?" our storekeeper asked. "He'd like some, wouldn't he?"

"No muskrat just now, either."

"Woodchuck? Rabbits?"

"No. They're all gone, too."

"Gosh, Peg. Gettin' kinda low, aren't you?"

My wife smiled. "Only temporarily. Ron will probably drag something new back with him tonight."

She was right. Ever since I buried a squashed caterpillar with full honors when I was four years old, I've been in the wildlife business. Not big things like lions and cobras, but little ones like orphan raccoons and turtles and blacksnakes and an oil-soaked loon.

My hobby of "collecting" wild critters—whether it's caring for those that have run afoul of man's ways, or getting to know others in their own surroundings—has always been a wonderfully rewarding one. And when Peg married me, she landed right in the middle of it.

I don't know why these things just seem to gravitate toward me.

1

But they do, wherever I go. Last June I gave a commencement speech at a small high school. As I stood in line with the brand-new graduates after the ceremonies, I murmured a polite "thank you" as each person commented on my talk. But the kid brother of one of the seniors brought me up short.

As I reached out my hand to grasp his, he seemed to hesitate and pull away. I grabbed for it with both hands, all smiles. Instantly I felt something scratchy and wiggly.

"That's my toad," said the owner of the knobby creature. "And what I want to know, Mr. Rood—kin they really give you warts?"

I suppose I have only myself to blame for such things, because I must admit I encourage them. But sometimes I like to shift a little of the blame—or credit—to a kindly gentleman who, himself, encouraged me nearly forty years ago. His name is Thornton W. Burgess.

Dad and I used to go for walks in the country near our Connecticut home. He'd show me how to decipher tracks in the dust, or how to tell a pine from a hemlock because the pine poked its tip up straight while the hemlock lopped over. One November day we came across a tiny turtle, so numb that it could hardly move.

"How come a turtle is walking around now?" I asked. "Shouldn't he be sleeping in the mud or something?"

Dad shrugged. "I don't know, Ronald. Why not write to Thornton Burgess? Maybe he'll have some ideas."

I did. And he had. Two full pages of them. Typewritten and single-spaced. The gist of it was that the little fellow had likely been wakened from hibernation by the warm sun.

At the end, the letter was signed by the great author-naturalist himself. The creator of Peter Rabbit, Jimmy Skunk and Old Mother West Wind had deigned to answer *me!*

That did it. From then on, there could be nothing better in this world than to be a naturalist.

Mr. Burgess used to have an evening radio talk. I listened well to what he had to say. On one occasion I listened too well. It got me in trouble all over the neighborhood.

"Tent caterpillars," he said, "have been worse orchard pests this past summer than ever before. If you have an apple or cherry tree, look for their egg masses. These are shiny little clusters wrapped around the twigs. If you can get rid of them you can help keep the tent caterpillars from spreading."

Next day I collared my pal Don Brown. "Have you heard about the tent caterpillars?" I asked. "They're going to wreck everybody's orchard."

"You mean they'll kill the apple and cherry trees? And peaches, too?"

"Yep. Unless we get rid of the eggs."

"But how do we do that?"

"You're supposed to find the egg clusters. They're easy to see, now that the leaves are gone. Then you put them in a big paper bag and burn them."

We decided to look into the possibility of saving Plymouth's hundreds of fruit trees, figuring that maybe we could get our friends to help us.

Especially were we worried about Old Tom's gnarled tree which hung so invitingly over a certain picket fence. We called it the "moonlight cherry" because of the mysterious raids on it that took place at night when the fruit was ripe. Loaded with huge Oxheart cherries in summer, it was a temptation to every boy in Plymouth. It was said that Old Tom kept a shotgun loaded with rock salt near his door. We only half-believed the rumor, but none of us wanted to test it. Not by daylight, anyway.

So every year when other folks complained that robins were getting their cherries, Tom had cause to complain loudest of all. Only it wasn't robins. More like owls, I guess—if there's any kind of owl that eats fruit.

Off we went to alert our neighborhood chums. Most of them were willing, especially when somebody pointed out that he'd heard there was a reward for every hundred egg clusters collected. The great tent-caterpillar hunt began.

Our orchard was rich with the brown-black, shellacked egg masses. Carefully Don and I snipped the little twigs that held them, or peeled them off the larger branches. Into a paper bag they went, for counting and sorting later. My friends did the same with theirs. We were to meet the following Saturday to consolidate our gains.

There was only one hitch. Saturday didn't come—at least not the one we had planned on. The first hundred egg masses came easy. So did the second. But after that, as the winter began to nip, we slowed down.

"How much money do they pay for each hundred clusters, Ron?"

"I don't know. Somebody thought twenty-five cents."

"Who's paying it?"

"I don't know that, either."

"It's cold out here. Let's go inside and warm up. We can pick more eggs tomorrow."

This must have been the general conversation around several other fruit trees, too. The eggs didn't seem such a good idea now that the sun was down. Then, boylike, we forgot the whole thing in the morning.

The eggs didn't forget, though. Sitting in their paper bags in half a dozen warm homes, they began to develop. After about two weeks at room temperature, the bags burgeoned like pregnant guppies. Thousands of tiny web-spinners made their way hungrily around the inside of their paper prisons until they found an exit.

One day Don took me aside at school. "Ronny, I don't think you'd better come over to my house tonight. Is my mother ever sore at you!"

"At me? What's the matter?"

"Worms. That's the matter. We're all over worms. You know the eggs we got week before last?"

"Oh, sure. How many did you get?"

"Too many. They hatched out and crawled all over the house. Up on the curtains. Down the table leg and over the floor. And each one of them laying out a little string of web as he went along."

"Gee. What'd your mother say?"

It wasn't what his mother had said that bothered him; it was what she'd made him do. He'd had to take the broom to the entire kitchen—walls, ceiling, everything. And much the same had happened in our neighbors' homes, too. One helper's mother had made him wash every dish in the cupboard. Another friend's father had made him wash the windows where the worms had crawled over them and left their silken webs.

As soon as school was out I rushed home. Our tremendous paper sack, thank goodness, had been almost shut. There were just a few dozen caterpillars crawling around on the outside of it. I took them out to the back shed. There the cold soon put an end to them and to my save-the-orchards campaign.

For the remainder of the winter I fancied myself an unwelcome guest at several neighborhood homes. But in the spring I was able to redeem myself. This was in the matter of the frog eggs.

Early in the spring the male and female frogs congregate in great numbers in the frigid waters of swamps and ponds. Not gifted with enough brains to be coy, the females kick and splash around until they are clasped around the waist by a male. Since a movement in the water may mean a female, the males dive and grab with their front legs at nearly everything that stirs. Sometimes this is another male. Then this outraged gentleman twists and struggles until he's free of the other's mistaken embrace.

Finally, trial-and-error gets the desired result. The male finds a female bursting with eggs. He grips her until she must feel like an hourglass. But neither of them has any external organs of sex, so they come to grips and little more. The eggs squeeze out like tapioca from a toothpaste tube and the male emits his sperm into the water.

The millions of tiny sperm cells, tails lashing, go out in all directions. A fortunate few find the eggs. Out of these, one penetrates each egg and a new amphibian life is launched.

The eggs are surrounded by a gelatinous envelope. This absorbs water until it has swelled many times its original size. We used to find these big blobs of jelly irresistible. Every spring we'd bring back jars and cans loaded with potential hundreds of frogs. Mrs. North allowed a few in her classroom; the rest generally ended up with me.

"Want some new-hatched tadpoles?" a pal asked one day.

"Yep," I replied.

"Nope," said Mother, who was listening. She knew I had a tub and two dishpans full of eggs and tadpoles already.

"Oh," said my friend. "But what'll I do with them? They're hungry and my mother won't let me keep any more than I have already."

He was desperate. I gave him a look that small boys all understand perfectly well. An hour later, when Mother had forgotten, we quietly eased another hundred little pollywogs into the turkey roaster.

Serving as a repository for all the frog eggs in the neighborhood helped me get out of the bad graces of the tent-caterpillar victims. For a while I tried to feed several thousand of the black little wigglers. I gathered old wood, stones and plant stems which were thick with algae for their scraping little mouths.

As they got larger, however, it became a discouraging task. Hungry for something to eat, they started on each other. The tail was the first to go. One day I saw a couple of dozen abbreviated little tadpoles waggling their way over the bottom like cocker spaniels trying to be friendly. The time had come, I knew, to let them go. Back to the swamp went the whole works, tailed and de-tailed.

The following year, after an early frog-egg hunt, I wrote my second letter to Thornton Burgess. Connecticut had been unusually warm during a February thaw, and I'd been looking hopefully for early frog eggs. Though I found none, I wondered what would happen after winter sleepers woke up during a thaw. "Will frogs and snakes know enough," I wrote to him, "to go back to sleep again when it gets cold, or will they starve?"

I remember his answer. It came over the radio.

"I have been asked what happens when hibernators wake up too early. Sometimes a snake will bask on a warm slab or rock until the sun drops behind the hills. Usually it is able to make its way underground again. Frogs and turtles sunning on a log may do the same thing."

But he went on to tell of other creatures who weren't this lucky, citing a listener's report of some ducks that had dropped into a patch of open water during the thaw, and somehow stayed too long. Now the weather had turned cold again, they were frozen in the ice.

"The game warden cannot rescue them because the ice is still too thin," he continued as we listened in horror. "So he throws corn across it for them to eat each day."

I thought of those ducks, their feet held fast by the ice. Then I turned to my father. "Oh, Daddy, Daddy, what will they do?"

Dad assured me that in a day or two the ice would be thick enough to hold the weight of a rescuer. "Besides, ducks spend all winter in the cold water, anyway," he said.

That night, as Jimmy, Irma and I went upstairs to bed, we listened to the whistle of winter, now back once more.

"I hope those ducks are in a sheltered spot," shivered Jimmy.

"Don't worry," our sister assured us. "If the water melted in the first place, it must be warm there all the time."

Comforted and hopeful, I climbed into bed. I tried not to hear the wind rattling the panes of the old farmhouse windows. After a while I dropped off to sleep.

Not all such stories have a happy ending, but this one did. In a day or two, Mr. Burgess told his audience, the game warden had been able to push a board out on the ice. Then he inched his way over it until he could chop the ducks free. A few days in a wire enclosure and they were in perfect shape again.

One of the reasons I rejoiced over the rescue was that we had three ducks of our own. We named them Lady, Quackie and Mr. Doozlin. They were of the Muscovy breed, and I'd been fast-talked into taking them off a friend's hands and paying for the privilege besides. Or so Dad claimed when they got out of their duckyard and went harvesting in the garden.

"Get those fool ducks back where they belong or somebody's going to have a duck dinner tomorrow!" he would roar.

Lady and Quackie were fine little ducks. Each brought off a fluffy brood of youngsters. But Mr. Doozlin—no doubt aided and assisted by us three delighted children—was a most surprising drake.

If you know Muscovy ducks at all, you know that they seldom quack. This is especially true of the males. Instead, they hiss. My sister, Irma, described their hiss as sounding like "someone trying to gargle in a whisper." Mr. Doozlin became my particular pet, although he was almost as big as I was, and hissed in a most convincing manner.

To bring out a fine hiss from him, all you had to do was stoop (or squat, for a seven-year-old like me) and pat his broad, glossy-green back. His tail would waggle with pleasure, and he'd stretch his neck forward again and again, hissing like a happy radiator.

Twelve-pounder though he was, Mr. Doozlin still managed to find his way out of the duckyard. Lady and Quackie could fly, but he was too portly and dignified for such antics. Instead he would search until he found a spot where the wire wasn't pegged down to earth securely, and out he'd go. Then he'd come walking across the lawn to whoever was handy, hissing and wagging his tail as if he deserved a round of applause.

When Mr. Doozlin was in his finest feather, a gentleman we'll call Mr. Jones was likewise in his. He sold drug and cosmetic products from door to door. If he happened to catch the lady

8

of the house at home, she'd be in for a good half-hour's harangue
—unless, of course, she bought something real quick in self-defense.
As a result, his sales record per call was phenomenal, although he
once told my mother she was the first woman he'd found at
home all morning.

Mother found his sales pitch fascinating. But then she was
always ready to listen—whether it was a house-to-house salesman
or a hobo. She'd listen sympathetically while a knight of the road
detailed his troubles to her, until finally her heart warmed to the
sandwich-and-coffee stage. And so Mr. Jones usually found her a
good customer, despite Dad's spluttering over every purchase she
made.

"You could buy the same stuff at half the price at the store,"
he'd say.

"But the poor man's got to make a living," she'd tell him.

One day when I was alone in the house, Mr. Jones drove into the
back yard. Mr. Doozlin met him at the car door, hissing and wagging in rare form.

Mr. Jones started to get out. Then he paused. He'd never met
a Muscovy drake before.

For quite a while he sat there. He pretended to busy himself
with some order blanks, but the old drake wouldn't go away.
Finally the car inched back out of the driveway and turned down
the street.

A day or so later, Mr. Jones happened to be talking in the village
store. "I called on every house from Plymouth to Terryville," he said,
"except the Roods'. And I'll be hanged if I'll set one foot out of the
car until they get rid of that blasted goose!"

Mr. Doozlin enjoyed full driveway privileges from that day on.

My Muscovy ducks were joined, during the two or three years
I had them, by other assorted pets. Some of these were harmless
creatures like somebody's leftover Easter chicks. Others were such
things as an alligator a friend had brought up from Florida.
There were two white rats, too, which one of my chums presented

9

to me at the insistence of his mother.

All of these laid the groundwork for the experiences of the years to follow. And while I had only one or two creatures at a time as a boy, now they may build up to as many as two dozen or more on occasion. And every one of them has given its own peculiar zest to my life as a "collector"—sometimes of animals themselves for a while, but more often of facts and incidents about their way of life.

So I really don't wonder that the storekeeper offered Peg a few free lettuce leaves with the groceries. If they weren't needed at the moment, they would be soon.

CHAPTER TWO

What Are Little Boys Made Of?

"HUMAN BEINGS," Don Brown read aloud, "are born with just two basic fears. One is the fear of loud noises. The other is the fear of falling. All other fears must be learned. This includes fear of fire, fear of getting hurt, and even the fear of snakes."

He put the book down. "See? I told you. People aren't naturally afraid of snakes. It's just because everybody else is, so they are, too."

I thought this revelation over for a minute. "Do you mean that a little baby isn't afraid of snakes?"

"Not according to this book."

"Not even a big one? Not even if it crawled right over his feet?"

"Nope."

We were kneeling down beside a pen in the back yard. Dad had taken us children to the Bronx Zoo early in the season, and I'd bought a fifty-cent Ditmars booklet which told about snakes. It made them sound so fascinating that Don and I caught a harmless garter snake on the strength of it. Together we learned about the amazing tongue which "sampled" the air for odors. We discovered the belly scutes which allowed the snake to glide over

11

the ground, and the peculiar jaw-hinge which enabled it to swallow relatively monstrous prey.

We became so engrossed that we forgot our own fears. Soon we captured more snakes. Finally we had over a dozen of them. Now, looking at the pen full of snakes basking peacefully in the sun, we decided that some day we'd see if the book was really right.

The chance came sooner than either of us suspected. A day or two later, we had visitors. "Now, Ronald, you watch Phillip and see that he keeps out of mischief," Mother said, shooing me out the back door with a damp little two-year-old. "His mother and I want to talk for a while."

I surveyed my small charge disdainfully. "Still in rubber pants," I grumbled. "And I'm stuck with the job of taking care of him."

Out onto the back lawn we went. Then I remembered Don Brown and his book.

I glanced back at the house. No sign of any adults. "Phillip," I said to him, "come with me."

Trustingly, the little fellow took my hand. I led him over to the edge of the snake pen. "These are nice, tame snakes," I purred. "How would you like to play with them?"

I'm not sure what he said, but it wouldn't have made any difference anyway. Quickly I picked him up and set him down right in the middle of my garter snakes.

He looked up at me in surprise. "It's all right," I nodded. "Go ahead. Play with them. See how smooth they are. Not slimy. See how much they like you, Phillip."

And lo, the book was right! Little Phillip had the time of his young life. He stroked the snakes thoughtfully as they lay in the sun. He picked them up and let them slide back to the ground. His eyes shone. Pleasure showed in his whole being as he sat among his new-found friends.

Everything was lovely. For five minutes, everything was wonderful. After that, things began to happen.

WHAT ARE LITTLE BOYS MADE OF?

First there was a noise. About one part scream and four parts bellow. Then, before I could turn around, there was a series of earth tremors. Phillip suddenly shot skyward, trailing snakes as he rose. At the same instant I was sent sprawling on the grass.

The earth whirled for a moment. Then my eyes came into focus. I saw the retreating form of Phillip's indignant mother, who had snatched her beloved from the jaws of death.

"Don't you ever play with my boy again!" she threatened. "Ever, ever, ever!"

And—you guessed it: Phil's been afraid of snakes ever since. I've been afraid of his mother, too.

That was my first big snake story. I remember another of a different sort. It involved a chicken farmer and a long, sleek blacksnake.

I was visiting Christy's chicken ranch. The owner was showing us around the place. "These chickens are two weeks old," he said. "We let them run free on the range here until they're big enough for broilers and fryers. Then we ship 'em to market and start all over again."

We walked a little farther and then his face darkened. "Oh, no!" he cried. "Not *another* one!" He strode forward to where a chicken struggled weakly by a watering trough. It had been attacked by something, and its side was bleeding. "That's the second one today. And two yesterday. And who knows how many more that I haven't found?"

Grimly he dispatched the wounded creature. "If I ever get my hands on what's killing those chickens . . ."

Now our eyes were alert for further evidence. We stopped near a suspicious bunch of feathers. I was just about to say something when he raised his hand in warning.

"Hush! There he is! The dirty, thieving, low-down *snake*!"

He rushed forward, tearing a slat from a brooderhouse as he ran. Then, like a man half crazy, he slashed and beat at something on the ground. It writhed and twisted to escape his blows, but could

13

barely move along, for its body was swollen with two great lumps.
It was a blacksnake, all of five feet in length.

Finally the snake lay still. Mr. Christy gave one last kick and
then looked at me. Panting from his exertion, he pulled out his
jackknife. "I'll show you, young fellow. You and your snakes.
By thunder, that blacksnake's murdered his last chicken!"

He bent down and slit the snake at the site of the incriminating
lumps. "Now we've got him red-handed . . ."

Then his mouth dropped in amazement. There, tumbled to the
ground in release from the snake's belly, were the bodies of the
real culprits—two full-grown, yellow-toothed rats.

It seldom happens in life that you can prove your point so
dramatically. And, of course, there are few things on this earth that
are all good or all bad. Blacksnakes, although they will follow
a rat right down in its hole, are certainly not above helping
themselves to fledgling birds when the chance offers itself. But
Mr. Christy summed it all up beautifully as he gazed at his dead
ally:

"You know," he said softly, "if I'd known what was inside that
snake, he could have had half a dozen chickens free. Snakes are
bad, but rats are worse."

There were many other creatures besides snakes that I got to
know on our portion of the Connecticut countryside. A few of these
were auto casualties we nursed back to health after they'd been
found by the roadside. One of these was a wood turtle we
called Brownie. She would prudently stay atop a little table for
hours while Spots, her water-turtle cousin, whom I'd brought home
for a weekend stay from a swamp, would unhesitatingly tumble
to earth from its edge. Apparently Brownie, being a dry-land turtle,
knew that a fall from the table might be disastrous, but Spots
launched fearlessly off, expecting the cushioning effect of water
below.

There was Mumps the chipmunk, who used to stuff his cheek-
pouches so full of sunflower seeds that he got stuck in his hole—

until Dad sneaked up and touched his struggling little behind. Then he made it, as Dad said, "like he was greased."

There was Grumbles, too.

Grumbles was an old warty toad, the largest I've ever seen. He lived under the foundation of the house, and came out each evening to look for insects. He'd creep up on a fly or beetle in a manner quite different from the usual hop of a toad. It was a stealthy crawl, first one foot and then another. Finally, when he was close enough, there'd be a flicker of movement—and the fly would be gone. Grumbles's long, sticky tongue, attached at the front of his mouth, was quicker than our eyes could follow.

Grumbles loved to have his back scratched. My sister and I used to take a blade of grass and tickle him with it. He'd twist and turn as Irma ran the grass along his side, as much as to say, "A little lower. Now a little to the left. Now toward the center. There—that's it!"

He used to sit on the ground under the kitchen window at night. There he'd stay as long as the light was on, happily picking up the insects which crashed against the lighted windowpane and fell down to where he waited. Sometimes they'd come so fast that he'd get behind in his tongue-work. The wings from one would still be showing at the corner of his mouth when another would drop down beside him. At such times, like a baby in a highchair, he'd toss all convention aside. Even while he was snapping at a new insect, he'd be stuffing the last one into his mouth with his front feet. Toads can live for months without food, I'm told, and Grumbles seemed to expect to have to do it for the next decade.

Although most of the animals I "collected" as a boy really had their freedom except as I poked into their affairs, there was one creature I wanted for a bona fide pet. This was a crow.

Dad had told me about a crow he'd had as a boy—how it would fly to his shoulder when he was plowing, how it would imitate him in a scratchy voice, and how it used to eat from the dish with his dog. It sounded to me as if a crow would be about as nice a pet as a boy could have.

Thus it was with unbounded glee that I accepted a friend's request one July day.

"I'm going to camp for two weeks, Ronny. How'd you like to take Inky while I'm gone?"

"Your crow? Oh, boy!"

So we made a place for Inky in the barn. At last I had a crow, even if for just two short weeks.

I also had a number of other things. Little, moving things. They came along as an added bonus.

Mostly they stayed with Inky. But a few of them did not. And it was these latter that gave me all the trouble.

I discovered them right after I'd put the big black bird on my shoulder. As I ran my fingers through his shiny feathers and pulled my hand away, along came a few dozen of his friends. Many-legged, dark and smaller than sand grains, the little bird mites immediately began to race up my wrist.

I gave my arm a violent shake. Inky squawked away to the other side of the barn. Rubbing furiously, I brushed off the little souvenirs he'd left me. Stripping off my shirt and scratching at my head, I fought real and imaginary mites while the crow watched in astonishment.

Finally I calmed down. After all, this was no way for an eleven-year-old boy to act who professed a fondness for everything that lived.

"Inky," I said, while the crow eyed me warily, "we've got to find you a little flea powder."

Dad had some fluoride powder he dusted on the chickens to keep them free of lice. So I enlisted Irma's help in dry-cleaning our crow.

"Just in case he should get lice from the barn," I said, not telling her the true reason. She was a bit squeamish about such things.

So while my sister held Inky, I doused him with what was probably enough powder for a dozen crows. When we finished, the indignant crow looked as if he'd been rattled around in a flour barrel.

I don't know if it was the powder or the pummeling that went with it, but this cured Inky's mites. I looked for them the next day. Not a one could I find.

The crow, thank goodness, was resilient enough to take it all in stride. He forgot his experience in a few hours. Soon he was eating bread soaked in milk and helping himself from a dish of hamburger.

Like many crows, Inky liked to collect bright objects. One of the barn windows had been broken and replaced; we found bits of the glass in a corner of the barn sometime later. We also discovered a ring that Irma had removed when we de-mited him, and which she couldn't find when we were through. The shell of a barn-swallow's egg completed the list.

One day a man came to see my father. "Dad will be back in a few minutes," I told him. "While you're waiting for him, would you like to see my crow?"

Being a guest, he found himself obliged to oblige, so I trotted ahead of him to the barn.

"He really belongs to a friend," I explained, handing the dubious crow-lover two pounds of feathered charm.

"Oh, is that so?" my visitor asked politely. "And what do crows eat, anyway?"

"Well, out in the wild they'll eat almost anything. Berries or bugs or meat. But we feed this one hamburger and cookies and milk."

I was about to say more, but Inky stopped me. My visitor had been warming up to the crow, stroking his plumage and smiling as much to encourage himself as to reassure the bird. And it was at this moment that Inky delivered his *coup de grâce*.

17

"Whack!" went that great black bill. Luckily, the man saw it coming, and rolled with the blow. Otherwise he would have lost a tooth.

On second thought, he had already lost it. Some time ago. And in its place was a fine gold crown. It was the gold that had attracted Inky's attention. He'd merely wanted it for his collection.

This was enough. My guest dropped the crow. Then the tooth showed again in a wan attempt at a smile.

"Thanks," he muttered, "for letting me see your crow. Now shall we see if your father has come home yet?"

He retreated without waiting for an answer. Later, as he talked with Dad, I could see that he'd keep running his tongue over that precious gold tooth. But he said nothing, for which I'm eternally grateful.

A few days later Inky went back to his rightful owner. Undoubtedly he has long since passed to his reward.

Having Inky for two weeks dulled my desire for a crow. Having him for two minutes probably did the same for my father's visitor.

I suppose I should have known better than to take the man up into the barn. But then, he should have known better than to follow me so willingly. After all, he'd once been a boy himself.

CHAPTER THREE

Forgotten Swamp

As THE MILES sped by, I felt a mounting excitement.

"Fifteen minutes more," I told the children. "Maybe twenty if the road is bad. Then we'll be there."

"Oh, boy. Flag Pole Swamp," exulted Alison.

"Flag *Hollow* Swamp," I corrected her.

"Did you really see a deer there? With her fawn?"

"Sure did, Janice."

"And you saw a bobcat there once, too?"

I told them once more of the thrill of facing the wildcat, its fangs bared in a soundless snarl, and how it faded into the swamp grass without moving a leaf. I recounted, too, the small-boy ecstasy as I stalked a painted turtle until, with a rush, the beautiful olive-and-orange creature was mine. I recalled again the hours I'd spent with my homemade microscope over a few drops of Flag Hollow water, peering at creatures right out of science fiction.

Now the moment was at hand. At last I was bringing my wife and children to see for themselves the wonderful swamp where I'd spent so many boyhood hours. As we rounded the last bend, I wondered if the swamp itself might be an anticlimax after all the stories I'd told them.

19

I needn't have worried. We slowed down at the little bridge that spanned Flag Hollow Brook at its lower end, and I realized that something was terribly and dreadfully wrong.

Numbly, I read the sign. "On this spot," it said, "will be located a modern new industrial plant. Completion by November. PROGRESS IN INDUSTRY FOR A BETTER AMERICA."

Tons of gravel lay over the bed of the little fawn which my sister and I had discovered years ago. Bulldozers snorted atop the sandy grave of my painted turtles. The old hollow maple where the raccoons nested was pushed off to one side. A single dragonfly darted above the new-poured concrete foundation, perhaps looking for the quiet pond that had given it birth.

We looked in silence. Then Roger spoke. "*That* was the swamp, Daddy? Right there where all the people are?"

I nodded. "Yes, Roger. Right where all the people are."

"But Daddy—how about all the muskrats and frogs and blackbirds? What did the people do about them?"

I couldn't find the words to tell him just what had happened there. "Well, they—— They had to go somewhere else."

Tom seized on my words at once. "I don't like this place, Daddy. Let's go where all the swamp animals and birds are."

I looked at his serious eight-year-old face. "Sure, Tom. Sure. We'll go there. Soon as we possibly can."

Then, grimly, as I yanked the car into gear: "I promise."

If there's one place in my boyhood world that stood apart from the others, it would undoubtedly be Flag Hollow Swamp.

To look at it from the road was to gaze down upon the steaming jungles, the Florida Everglades, the African veldt. To listen to it was to be transported to a Carolina frog-marsh, an Iowa grasshopper-prairie or an Arctic tundra, depending on the time of the year. To breathe deeply of its air was to whiff a bit of Georgia's Okefenokee, Oregon's Malheur and—so Dad said—Connecticut's mud-flats at low tide. And to balance your way across its waters from one hummock to another was a trip, undoubtedly, toward Mecca.

I have heard it said that the trouble with youth is that it's wasted on kids. This was undoubtedly so in my case, too—most of the time. Not, however, during the times I spent at Flag Hollow. I savored every moment as if it were some rare, fine delicacy. I spoke to the swamp's many denizens, even called them by name.

There was Old Foxy, for instance, the painted turtle who used to sun himself on the big hummock at the west edge of the swamp. He seemed to know that, however many other turtles I caught, I would never disturb him, for a redwing's nest was on the hummock, too. Another turtle I called Spots was strangely tame—a little Eastern spotted turtle who allowed herself to be picked up whenever I chanced to come across her. There were also Stripes, Blump and Jerry. These were a ribbon snake, a green frog and a muskrat, respectively.

My swamp was iced over when, a few weeks before Christmas one year, my sister handed me a piece of paper. Irma was two years older than my eleven years, and was forever thinking up new schemes. Somehow she always persuaded Jimmy and me to join in them.

"I'm the mother," she said, "and you are my children. Now you make a list of things you want for Christmas, and I'll see what I can do about them."

Jimmy and I put down the usual small-boy things such as toys, wagons and Erector sets. Then I thought of my swamp.

"Hip boots," I printed in my best letters.

Dutiful little mother that she was, Irma took the list to our parents. Mother and Dad got the hint. This probably wasn't hard, for they knew full well of my love for Flag Hollow. In fact, now that I look back, I realize that many a lawn got mowed, many a garden weeded in record time, just so I could go down to "the swamp." At any rate, there was a box by the tree on Christmas morning and in it were my boots, black and wonderful.

It was a long winter. My boots stayed in their box, waiting for the day the ice would clear away from the water of the swamp. I tried them out during a January thaw in a mud puddle. Then I set them aside until spring.

Finally the day came. The Connecticut sun felt warm and strong, "hot enough to give you a suntan, Mom," I said as I came home from school. The silence of the March afternoon was punctuated by the swish of bits of snow and ice falling into the road. Little rivers of muddy water ran down the driveway.

Jimmy picked up the worn overshoes which he'd inherited when I got my boots, and we started for the swamp. The water had risen over the decaying ice, and I cautiously poked my feet down through the slushy stuff.

What a sensation it was as I stepped knee-deep into the water! Nobody had ever told me of the delightful way rubber boots wrinkle as they are forced against your legs by water pressure. Now I discovered this for the first time. Deeper and deeper I went, feeling the pressure creep up, higher and tighter. Highly elated and a little awe-struck, I walked slowly and carefully in my new world. I was an explorer. I was an adventurer. I was Columbus himself.

After my little brother's begging finally penetrated my consciousness, I let him have a try. Then, after I had a final wade, we took the boots home. But I was back the next day, and the next, enjoying my boots—quite literally and figuratively—to the brim.

Before getting real boots I had always teetered precariously from one tussock to another. I could seldom stay long in any one spot, for the spot would begin to sink and the water would creep up around the old overshoes. Now, however, I could take my stand on a hummock and slowly descend with no thought of wet feet. Better than that, I could step off into the water and for the first time be on the same level with my friends of the marsh.

Now I saw my watery world through completely different eyes.

22

FORGOTTEN SWAMP

If you want to have something of the same sensation, try going into the oil pit of a garage sometime. From above, most cars look like sleek creations of chrome, metal and glass. Now, from below, they look like rods and wires and braces and mud. Before, if you viewed them with an air of complete detachment, they ran effortlessly, mysteriously. Now, seen from a working angle, they ran because this gadget here attached to the wheels there, and this rod over here connected to that lever there.

The same was true of my swamp seen from a new angle. Squatting down on a slowly sinking hummock—sometimes for so long that I got a sudden cool wetness to the seat of my pants— or standing in water as deep as I dared, I became initiated into what really goes on in a marsh.

One of my first discoveries was in the form of a little water-shrew. No larger than a mouse, and sometimes smaller, these tiny creatures include among their numbers the world's smallest mammals. I recall measuring an adult masked shrew years later; its body was just over two inches long, plus a one-inch tail. It weighed less than half an ounce on our postage-stamp scales.

My Flag Hollow specimen, however, was the first shrew I'd ever seen. From the moment I saw it I was astonished. Not only was it mouselike and quick, but it did an incredible thing: it actually walked on the water.

I blinked in amazement, not knowing whether to believe my eyes. The little shrew, intent on stuffing its stomach with insects and tiny creatures found at the water's edge, paid no attention to me. It ran beneath the overhanging grasses, out across a little pool and over to the base of an old dead tree—all on top of the water. Then it disappeared beneath the surface.

I was just getting myself well convinced that I'd been the victim of some strange delusion when the shrew reappeared. Bone dry despite its subsurface jaunt, it immediately began its strange water ballet again.

Bending over until my eyes were almost level with the little creature, I determined to fathom the secret of his witchery. The dryness of his fur was easy to understand: he poked beneath the surface here and there but the fur was so dense that the water rolled off it as soon as he came up again.

The secret of water-walking, however, eluded me completely. I saw water-shrews many times in my summers at the swamp, but never was able to discover how they could seemingly defy the laws of nature. It wasn't until my biology teacher explained it a few years later in high school that I understood.

Mr. Jay had been talking about the Insectivores, that primitive group of creatures to which the shrews belong.

"I know you'll think it's funny," I said when he noted my upraised hand, "but I could swear I've seen shrews running right on top of the water. Can you tell me how they do it?"

In reply, he opened a book on his desk. "Here's your answer," he said, pointing to a picture. "See those stiff hairs on each of the water-shrew's feet? Every time the shrew takes a step, those hairs catch and hold a bubble of air. So it can run around on the water as if it were on four little basketballs."

There were other divers in my swamp besides the shrew that never got wet. One of these was the water boatman. Looking like a half-inch underwater rowboat, this little insect swam in the water with two long oarlike feet. It often floated at the surface until I startled it; then it dived beneath the water with jerky thrusts of its oars. Hairs on its body carried some of the surface air down with them, so it seemed encased in silver as it swam in its own air pocket.

Another diver was the water-spider. Long-legged, hairy, it even went so far as to build its nest below the surface. I came across many of them—silken networks that held a big bubble brought down piecemeal by the spider in the form of little scoops of air. Here, in the strange underwater nursery, she would weave her egg sac and raise her young.

There was hardly a visit to the swamp that didn't net me a

new acquaintance. I got to know the back-swimmers—those strange insects that spend most of their lives swimming upside down. I met the water-striders as they skated over the surface, their long slender feet making little dimples as they moved. I saw the snorkels of mosquito larvae as they hung, head downward, from the surface film, and took air in through a little rear-end tube. I even found where my little spotted turtle laid her eggs—on a sandy slope to the west of the swamp.

One day Irma came out to where I was mowing the lawn. She had my mother's binoculars. "Ronny," she said, "come with me. Down to the swamp."

"Why, what'd you find?" I asked.

Irma only smiled. "I'm not sure if it's anything at all. But I want you to look and see if it's what I think it is."

I parked the lawnmower under the cherry tree and moved to get my boots.

"No," she said with a firmness that surprised me. She tapped the binoculars. "These, yes. But no boots."

Perplexed, I tried to question her further. But she loved mysteries and wouldn't tell me any more. "You'll see," was all she would say.

I trotted along beside her until we got to the road that edged the swamp. Her pace slackened to a slow walk as she peered ahead. Finally she stood stock-still. "Now look," she said, handing me the binoculars. "Over at the far edge. Near that clump of bushes."

I could see a reddish-brown, lumpy object. It looked to be part of a hummock, but I knew my swamp well enough to realize it was something I'd never seen before.

"What do you think it is?" my sister asked as I squinted through the glasses.

"Golly, Irma. Do you really think so—do you really think it's a deer?"

She was jubilant. "Yes I do, Ronny. It's a mother deer. And she has a tiny fawn right with her. I saw it before."

Dad had taught us how to make a long, low whistle. Not enough to frighten an animal, but enough to cause a woodchuck to stand up in curiosity, or to stop a fleeing animal in its tracks. "I'm going to whistle," I said.

"All right, but quietly. We don't want to scare her."

When I whistled, the effect was immediate. We'd been screened somewhat from the doe by the bushes at the edge of the road; now she raised her head and looked in our direction. Two great ears pointed out like the sound-scoops they were. At the same time, a tiny mottled red-and-white head raised itself from the grass. It seemed no larger than the head of a dachshund.

"Gosh, the fawn doesn't look as if it'd weigh more than five pounds," I whispered.

We watched it a few minutes more, then slowly backed away until we were safely out of sight. "Now, don't you tell anybody," said Irma. "Anybody at all. This will be our own secret. All right?"

I swore eternal silence. It was a tremendous temptation to let my pals in on the secret, but I managed to contain myself.

Daily I sneaked down to the swamp with the binoculars, but the doe did not appear again. Knowing, somehow, that her large bulky body would appear conspicuous while that of her spotted offspring would camouflage itself perfectly in the grass, she remained away during the daytime. But I could see the matted place at the edge of the hummock where she pulled herself out of the water at dusk to feed her fawn, so I knew he was still hiding there.

They remained in their watery fortress for about a week. Then one day the matted grass no longer was closely slicked down and I knew the little family had gone. Giving them a few more days' grace, I finally waded out to the hummock. There was the "form" in the grass where the little fellow had lain, but no sign that his mother had ever rested there. Later I learned that fawns have no scent when very young, so his mother had been protecting him by her very absence.

26

FORGOTTEN SWAMP

Since that first experience with deer, I've found fawns two more times—once in a hemlock thicket along a stream and once beneath a low-hanging cherry tree at the edge of an old pasture. But never do I expect to find a fawn more perfectly hidden than my little Flag Hollow friend—right out in the open on five feet of land, surrounded by water on all sides.

My rubber boots transported me to every part of the swamp. They helped me catch Old Foxy, the painted turtle who'd always eluded capture until I was able to sneak up on him through the water from the rear. They allowed me to tread the mud carefully where a frog had dived in, until I touched the surprised creature and made him find a new hiding place. They took me right up to Jerry the muskrat's domed house of reeds so I could inspect its underwater entrance.

My real discovery, however, came without boots. In fact it arrived in an old tin can. I used to stop at the swamp on my way home from school. Sometimes one of my friends would be with me; we'd collect little yellow-bellied salamanders to take home for a few days. On this particular afternoon, however, I was alone. I saw Blump in his usual place on the log, his green skin glistening and his froggy eyes bulging as he waited for an unwary fly.

I picked up an old can that had been tossed by the roadside, laid down my lunch pail, and sneaked up on Blump. When I got close enough, I pounced on him. He croaked and struggled, but I stuffed him in the can. As an afterthought I crammed in a little mud and grass, and filled the can with water.

It was this afterthought that made all the difference. For it opened up an entire new world: a world even now being explored by men and women in a hundred different lands, and into which I still inquire, some thirty years later. This is the world of the little things. It is the miscroscopic life all around us, responsible for many of our diseases, much of our crop success or failure and even—if present studies of microscopic algae bear their expected fruit—the food for future human generations. And I was introduced to it by a frog.

It came about because I put Blump in a big goldfish bowl. Into the bowl went the frog—mud, grass and all. He kicked and made such a commotion that I soon realized I'd never be able to keep him. I reached into the bowl, picked him out, and carried him back to the swamp in a jar.

When I got back, my new world was waiting for me. The swirling water was calm, and the mud had settled to the bottom. "Look," I said to Mother, "there's a little red spider swimming through the water. And look—there's a lot of little things that look like the poppyseeds on your rolls. And here's something crawling like a snail, only faster. And there's a green thing on the glass like a little octopus, with tentacles and all."

Mother paused in her work. She was never too busy to take an interest in our discoveries, for she loved the outdoors and its creatures, big and small. Sometimes she'd even shoo a mosquito off her arm rather than swat it. Now she sat down and looked into the water with me.

"What a lot of things! I wonder what they are."

She found a magnifying glass for me, and I stared into this strange new world. I got out what few books I had and figured out what its inhabitants must be. The red "spider" was an aquatic mite, I discovered. The "poppyseeds" were *Cladocera*—tiny swimming relatives of the crab and lobster. The snaillike creature was a planarian, harmless cousin of the tapeworm. And the green "octopus" was a hydra, freshwater relative of the jellyfish and corals.

The next day I showed my discovery to Don Brown. "If only I had a microscope," I said, "I could get a good look at these creatures."

"Why not make one?" he said.

"How do you do that?"

"Drill a tiny hole in a strip of tin, about the size of a pencil-lead. Smooth your hole off good with a file. Put a drop of water in the hole for a lens—and there's your microscope. I read it in a magazine."

We found the copy of the magazine and followed the directions. They worked wonderfully. We used a strip of tin about four inches long and an inch wide, with the corners rounded off. The hole for the lens was made near one end with a 1/16-inch drill. When we put a drop of water in the hole, it balled up into a tiny, transparent lens.

Placing a drop of swamp water on a glass platform over a hole in a box containing a small electric light, we poised our microscope over it and entered our invisible world. We watched the exquisite transparency of *Vorticella,* which looked like a tiny wineglass on a spiral stem. We saw ciliates row themselves through the water with thousands of tiny beating hairs. We marveled at the flow of an amoeba as it slid through its water-drop world, engulfing other creatures smaller than itself by oozing around them until they were surrounded.

We gathered new material from various parts of the swamp. Hour upon hour we spent until our necks were tired, bending over our peephole into the unseen. Later we both bought cheap microscopes and put the crude lens away. But the thrill has never departed. Now, as a biology teacher in a modern high school, I have access to two dozen precision 'scopes. And my idea of perfect relaxation is to take a scoop of gunk from a swamp and look at it through a microscope. I guess a naturalist is really a little boy who never grew up.

I enjoyed my swamp all through my school years. During the winters, my pals and I sometimes took apples to Jerry Muskrat, as we'd named him after a Thornton Burgess character. In spring we listened for the first spring peeper—that little frog whose cheerful, high-pitched note belied the ice water in which he did his mating. In the summer we'd catch turtles by the half dozen, or peek carefully into a bird's nest in a low bush. In the fall we'd listen to the buzz-chorus of ten thousand crickets and grasshoppers, singing furiously until the killer frosts numbed them forever. The day came when the rubber boots were too small even for Jimmy to wear. In another few years I went off to college. But my enthusiasm for the swamp scarcely dimmed; I visited it on holidays and during the summer.

During the war years I saw the swamp only on rare occasions. Then, after Germany and Japan were vanquished, I had my own life to live with Peg and the kids, many miles from my boyhood home in Plymouth.

Finally came that day of my return. Now I had Peg and our four beloved children. What memories came to me as we rounded the last corner before Flag Hollow Swamp!

——And then that terrible letdown. The bulldozers, the men with blueprints and measuring tapes, walking over the area where the redwings had called and the water had sparkled. With all the dry land in the United States, it had been thought necessary to fill in these two tiny acres of swampland.

"PROGRESS IN INDUSTRY FOR A BETTER AMERICA," said the sign which proclaimed the change.

Better for whom?

CHAPTER FOUR

One Acre of Raccoons

OUR FAMILY used to picnic with our friends the Lakes in the summer. After lunch—while Dad fished, Mother and Mrs. Lake talked or looked for birds, and Irma and Jimmy played with the Lake kids—I would trot along beside Mr. Lake as he explored the countryside. Although he'd never had any formal training as a naturalist, he possessed a keen interest in all the outdoors.

"You'll find in life," he'd say, pausing beside an ancient tree, "just what you want to find." Then he'd reach out and pull off a bit of bark. "See? A little world right in my hand. Gray lichens on the outside. And on the inside you see those tiny gray insects. Springtails, they're called, because they skip around. And here's a flat little wood centipede. And the egg case of a spider."

And so it would go, on through the woods. Season after season I'd watch him as he carefully parted the grass for a quick glance at a song-sparrow's nest, or knocked out his pipe thoughtfully as he squinted skyward at a hawk.

Indian arrowheads were his specialty. He had an astounding knack of finding them. We'd be walking along a path when he'd suddenly stoop down. "Not bad," he'd say, picking up a bit of stone. "But it'd be better if the point hadn't been broken off." And with that he'd hand it to me.

It made no difference if I'd walked the same path dozens of times before. I wouldn't have seen an arrowhead if it had come streaking out of ambush at the end of a wooden shaft. But let Lou Lake just amble the path once, and arrowheads would jump out of the dirt and lie there flopping until he picked them up.

I guess that's the way with almost anything that's of special interest to us. Buy a red convertible and you're suddenly struck by how many red convertibles there are on the roads nowadays. Put a fancy lamp-post in your front yard and you discover how many other people have fancy posts, too. A dog on a crowded street sees only other dogs, a woman with a new hat sees only other hats—and so on.

I never became aware of arrowheads enough to be good at finding them, but as my consciousness of the world of nature grew, so did the opportunities to delve into it even more deeply. Thus it was no surprise to me when I happened to go to college to find a hundred raccoons living in pens just off the campus. Nor was I surprised to discover that a position was open for a caretaker. After all, I was interested in such things. There lay the job in my path, just flopping like one of Mr. Lake's arrowheads until I took it up.

The college was the University of Connecticut. The raccoons were the property of the state, to be used as part of a 'coon stocking program. Raccoons had retreated with the advance of civilization. Now the state was trying to re-establish them. 'Coon care was provided by Forestry students such as myself, who gained experience plus a little cash as well.

"Well, Ronald, there they are," said my Forestry professor, indicating several dozen wire pens in a grove of trees behind his house. About eight feet long and three feet in height and width, they were built up on legs so they'd be off the ground. At one end they were closed in to provide a dark nest for the occupants.

"Norm Wilder will be along in a few minutes," he continued. "He'll show you around. Right now you can get acquainted. I have a class in ten minutes." Whereupon he walked off toward his car.

I glanced around for Norm. Not a sign of anybody yet. Just me and an acre of raccoons. And all of them out in their wire runways, looking at me.

"Well," I told myself, "you wanted the job, and here it is. Better start saying 'hello.' "

I found a barrel of food nuggets and placed a few of them in my pocket. Then I walked over to a cage on which was written "Skip." "Here, Skip," I said, gingerly presenting him with a nugget. Reaching out with his black little hands, he pulled it back through the wire.

I was elated. "You and I are going to get along just fine," I spoke aloud to two hundred listening ears. I watched as Skip backed up to the wire and began nibbling his morsel. Idly I stuck a finger in to tickle his fur.

At that moment I had my first lesson in raccoon anatomy. They're two-ended. And both ends are armed with teeth. Or so it seemed as Skip combined an about-face, a snarl and a snap all in the same instant.

"Quick, aren't they?" a voice asked as I recoiled just in time. "Even in a cage, they're still wild animals.

"I'm Norm Wilder," my new companion said. "Grad student in Wildlife." Then he held out a pair of heavy leather gloves. "Here. We don't often use these. Only if we have to handle the 'coons. Or," he grinned, "if we try to pet the wrong ones."

"You mean there are *right* ones?"

"Oh, sure. 'Coons are like people. Or like any other animal, for that matter. Each one is an individual. Here—let me show you around."

The "showing around" took a little longer than it was meant to. It began that fall and was still going on late the next spring. The raccoon doesn't wear that black face-mask for nothing: behind it hides a delightful personality. And with a hundred masks to decipher, we never got to know them all.

One of the most unforgettable of the 'coons was a portly gentleman by the name of Cubby. He was the largest specimen I've ever seen—weighing something over twenty pounds, as I recall. Cubby was a terror to the others, even if he was caged by himself. A snarl from him would send the animals in neighboring cages racing for their nest-boxes. One night he got out and panicked the whole 'coonery, tearing at the wire mesh of other cages and creating a general ruckus.

"I pity the 'coon dog that tangles with Cubby," Norm said as we watched our oversized charge hurl insults at a neighboring nest-box. "Too bad he's so sour on the world. It'd be nice to mate him and get a few more tough eggs like him."

"Yes," I agreed. "But he lights so fast into anything that moves that he'd kill a female before he even found out she was a lady."

So Cubby continued unloved and childless. Then one morning our professor had news for us. "Never heard such a commotion as there was out in the pens during the night," he said. "Sounded as if someone had brought a tomcat to a dog show. Kept me awake half the night."

We raced out to the pens. Everything seemed in perfect order—until we came to Cubby's box. Somehow he'd worked the catch loose and pushed the door open. There was no sign of him anywhere.

"Oh, no!" gasped Norm. "Cubby's gone. That's what all the fuss was about. He probably cussed the whole place out before he took off for the woods. Bet we never see *him* again."

Glumly we continued our rounds, feeding and watering the remaining ninety-nine. We'd gotten sort of to love the grumpy old fellow, and hated to think we'd let him escape.

But we needn't have worried. The last row of cages was our catch-all section. It contained several groups of youngsters, one old toothless female, and a few unmated lady 'coons as well. And here, in the corner of the cage of our prized black female—was Cubby.

It was easy to reconstruct the story. He'd made his swaggering way to the co-ed section. Blacky's cage must have been right in his way, or perhaps the little female had made the mistake of not hiding when his lordship put in an appearance. At any rate, Cubby had decided that this, of all cages, suited him better than his own bachelor's quarters. So, with teeth and claws, he'd finally forced his way inside.

There was only one hitch. Blacky didn't retreat. Cubby's tattered left ear showed that. So did a missing patch of fur on his side. Scarcely half the size of the big male, she had finally given him his comeuppance.

We glanced at the wire which had swung in to allow Cubby to enter, but which cut off his retreat. "There, you big bully," Norm said as he fastened it shut. "Maybe you've met your match."

Cubby gave a pleading whimper. Blacky snarled him to silence. Norm repaired the wire on the peppery little lady's cage. She, in turn, rushed at his gloved hands, mad in her new-found power.

And so Cubby found his mate. Perhaps some of the gentle sex who read these words will nod wisely, saying, "Of course—it just took the feminine touch, that's all." There's one last little bit to add to the story, though. After observing the newlyweds for about a week, one of the Forestry students quietly took a heavy black pencil out to the cage with him. Carefully he crossed out "Blacky" on the cage's tag. In its place he wrote a name that stayed with her from then on: "Spitfire."

Cubby wasn't the only wanderer. Raccoons are so inquisitive, so ready to investigate everything with those clever hands, that we almost felt as if padlocks would be the only things that would keep them in place. And coupled with that curiosity is a neat capacity for sizing up a situation. I learned about this one day when Billy got away.

Billy was a raccoon we had recently acquired, having been captured in a trap set by a farmer who had been losing chickens.

Billy was still very wild and fearful of man. He'd spend most of the time in his nest-box, coming out only to eat. We got so used to seeing him curled up in his box that one day I forgot to lock the cage door, and only snapped it shut.

Of course this was all Billy needed. During the night he investigated the door. It was probably no more complicated than the entrance to the farmer's chickenhouse, and he soon made his escape. However, sensing perhaps that there were dogs and human habitations in almost every direction, he didn't bolt for freedom but merely scuttled up into a nearby hickory tree. Billy had taken his stand out as far as he could go in the topmost branch.

Norm groaned. "How'll we ever get him down?"

"Don't worry," I volunteered helpfully, "he'll come down when he's hungry. The only other way'd be for someone to climb up and get him . . ."

My voice trailed off as I realized what I'd said—and as I saw the gleam in the eyes of my professor and the graduate student. "Besides," I added lamely, "there's no ladder."

But a ladder was found. And in a few minutes I was swaying in the top of the hickory tree, with a net hanging from my belt in the best big-game-hunter tradition.

Billy watched me approach. His beady eyes never left me for a moment. Raccoons are as much at home in the trees as they are on the ground, and I didn't relish the thought of having it out with a desperate 'coon fifty feet in the air.

Then, as I inched closer, Billy decided to play hard to get. Slowly I stretched the net out toward him, as if somehow I expected him to jump into it like a nightgown-clad escaper from a hotel fire. He tucked his head between his paws and closed his eyes.

And there he was. And there I was. Stalemate.

By now there were a half a dozen people on the ground. All of them were as helpful as could be.

"Shake him loose!" called one. I tried to figure which of the three hands I needed could be spared to shake a clinging raccoon loose.

"Hook him off with the net," shouted another.

"Climb out on the limb," chortled still another, and I nearly threw the net down on him.

Finally still another student came running. "Here, Ron," he cried, brandishing a handsaw. "Cut the limb off and carry it down—raccoon and all."

By now I was strongly tempted to have someone call the fire department rescue squad, but the challenge of Billy was too great. So I descended and got the saw. Then I went back up and cut the limb off the tree. Then, inch by labored inch, I lowered him down, past other limbs, until I was at the top of the ladder.

"Easy does it," breathed Norm, who stood by with the large net, into which I would lower Billy in a few seconds. "Six feet more and he's ours."

What happened next makes me wince even now, some twenty years later. Anybody who knows wild animals should have known it would happen. Certainly I should have expected it, after all the stunts the raccoons had pulled in the past. Billy suddenly came to life.

In one smooth motion he raised his head, glanced around, and launched himself right into the middle of the ground crew. Scattering students in all directions, he headed for the nearest tree. He scrambled up it in a shower of bark. And in a twinkling he was in the same situation—except forty feet more to the west —that he'd occupied two hours before.

On the ladder I was having my own problems. The sudden release of the raccoon's weight, coupled with the force of his jump as he left the branch, completely upset me. I had been descending with my back to the tree, as one would go down a set of stairs. Now I dropped everything and clutched wildly at the ladder. But my grip failed, and I hit every rung all the way down with my heels and various other parts of my anatomy.

After I landed, not a word was said—audibly. Sadly we packed up our 'coon-catching outfit. Billy paid no attention to the operations below. Nevertheless we left food and water for him in his cage. Then we set a live-trap at the base of the tree in hopes that he'd walk into it. But he stayed motionless up there all day, and the next he was gone. We never saw him again.

Billy taught me something about raccoon canniness. I learned other 'coon characteristics as well. We were familiar with the way that raccoons wash their food—a trait that's celebrated in their scientific name *Procyon lotor,* meaning "the one who washes."

We had one raccoon who was so persistent in this regard that we finally gave up and called him Lotor. Once we gave him hamburger and oatmeal mixed, just to see him take it to the dish of water and wash it until it had fallen apart and he couldn't find it any more.

"To know why a raccoon washes its food, you'd have to be a raccoon yourself," we were told in Wildlife class. "But it must be related to their delicate sense of touch. Certainly the raccoon must feel its food better with wet hands than with dry. A raccoon will even wash a fish."

The food our raccoons got was in half-inch pellets. It contained meat, bone meal and other assorted foods to approximate the widely varied diet—from berries to bugs—that raccoons take in the wild. Sometimes they would wash the rounded pellets so vigorously that they'd fly out of the dish and we'd have to pick them off the ground later.

Our two favorites were a couple of roly-poly twins we called Lum and Abner. They'd been named after the famous old radio characters. They got in about as much trouble, too, as their original namesakes used to do. We weren't supposed to make pets of any of the animals, but these two 'coons were exceptions. They were just too friendly to keep in a pen. So we'd often open the cage and let them wander while we fed the rest of the animals.

Abner had a double supply of raccoon curiosity. You could see the question marks hanging over his head in the manner of comic strips. If you sat down on the warm grass with Abner in your lap, his little hands would search you from head to toe.

Every pocket would be emptied, every button felt of, every fold of clothing investigated. If he could have figured the combination to the clasp, he'd have swiped my wristwatch. Rings, necklaces, earrings, fountain pens, belts—all of these on various visitors came under his ten-fingered scrutiny. And even while those little hands were searching, he'd be sniffing and looking to see what to poke at next.

Perhaps Abner had the curiosity that should have belonged to Lum as well, for Lum might fiddle with a button or shirt pocket for a moment and then go sound asleep in your lap. He was a great one to bask in the sun, despite the fact that raccoons are strongly nocturnal. Hence, when we let the two of them out, we could readily find them again, for Lum would be curled up in the nearest patch of sunlight, while a clatter would lead us to Abner as he investigated a tin can.

One day I was feeding my charges when a car drove into the yard. In it was a young professor, his wife and their infant girl. The professor came over to see the raccoons while his wife went into the house. I showed my guest around, introducing him to Cubby and Spitfire, George and Beulah, Three-Toes, Skip, Lotor and all the rest. "But our favorites," I said, glancing around, "are Lum and Abner."

"Oh? And which are they?"

"Well, they're here somewhere. We let them wander around while we're feeding the others. Tame as kittens, both of them. Tell you what—why don't you look over in that row, and I'll look down here. If you see a raccoon loose, it'll be one or the other."

So we started on our search. I was confident that they'd be found in less than a minute.

And so they were. The first inkling I had that they'd been located was a loud shriek.

"Frank! Frank! For heaven's sake, come here! There's one of those *beasts* in the car!"

Frank and I both hit the path on a run. Mrs. Frank was standing back from the car in horror, clutching her baby as if she were being attacked by wolves. On the back of the seat I could make out a raccoon, shuffling along as he investigated the upholstery.

Quickly I reached into the car. Abner whickered his little friendship call, and allowed me to pick him up. "Now, you nosey little critter," I told him, "there's no need to go into every car door that's open."

Luckily, the car was all right. I could glimpse the baby's basket and a pillow in the rear seat. Thank heavens Abner hadn't yet made it that far. Smiling what I hoped was my pleasantest smile, I tried to convince the professor's wife that it's perfectly normal to have a raccoon in the car. But she took a dim view of Abner, no matter how cute he was supposed to be.

Finally she got into the car. Just as they were about to drive away, my eye caught a movement in the back seat.

"Oh, by the way," I began, stalling for time as I peered more closely, "did you know that Abner has a twin brother?"

The professor's wife looked at me and guessed in an instant the reason for the question. Wordless, she vacated the car as if it contained a time bomb.

I opened the back door. My suspicions were confirmed. The "pillow" I'd seen before raised its head. Blinking pleasantly, Lum grunted at me from his perch on the rear seat.

They drove away, leaving me still holding the drowsy little fellow. From that time on, we were more careful with the twins, especially when there were guests present.

I learned to love raccoons during that year in college. They seem to take so readily to captivity if captured young that they're often kept as pets. Automatically housebroken, they're clean in all their habits. They will eat almost anything, and seem to thrive on canned dog food.

Their one consuming drive is curiosity. A raccoon will investigate almost anything. Those black little hands will feel your face, your buttons, your wristwatch. Take off your shoe and the raccoon will feel clear down to the toe. "Curious as a pet 'coon," according to the old saying, raccoons have turned hunting camps upside down when they've made their way inside.

Occasionally, as I cleaned the raccoon cages in the rain or nursed a nipped finger, I considered the possibility that there might be something else you could do to earn your way through college.

But none of them would be more fun. Not for me at least, when, like Mr. Lake and his arrowheads, I seemed destined to find wild critters in my path wherever I went.

CHAPTER FIVE

Chasing Ghosts

PEG—she was then Peggy Bruce—was my assistant in daily chores at the raccoon ranch. She helped me clean the cages and keep the records. She was invaluable in showing visitors around ("Better let me have that baby raccoon now, Mrs. Drake. I think I saw a flea on him—and your fur coat, you know . . ."), and she was astonishingly quick with the net in rounding up strays.

"You can out-think any raccoon in the place," I told her one day after a particularly exhilarating chase. And, good girl that she was, she took it as the highest compliment a tongue-tied Wildlife student could possibly muster.

She was handy at netting all kinds of quarry. Soon after I graduated I found myself asking her to be my wife. The request was so unexpected, she said, that there was no choice but to say yes. And so a Connecticut romance which began amid the musky aroma of the animal cages at Storrs, finally flowered a couple of years later at Stamford.

And it's been bearing the oddest fruit ever since. Not, I hasten to add, in terms of our four children, but in terms of what happens when an incorrigible nature-lover teams up with someone who's good with the net.

For a while even the world of nature had to wait, for this was the time of World War II. Peg joined the Marines and I joined the Air Force. Then, some four year later, we were back together again. And almost at once it began.

"You mean they actually pay good money for mosquitoes and things like that?" Peg asked me one night when I brought home a list with names of plants and animals on it. "Those biological supply houses must be crazy."

"Well, crazy or not, they keep 'em in stock so they can be used by colleges and laboratories for study. Listen to what they need: mosquitoes, grasshoppers, cockroaches, snails . . ."

"Ugh! Don't they want anything nice, like coconuts from a tropic isle, or maybe seashells from the Riviera?"

"Well, it says here that they'll give twenty cents each for ghost crabs."

"You mean those white scuttery things that ran all over the sand after dark when we were stationed down in Florida? That's more like it."

At first we were both fooling. But soon an excuse for a Florida vacation began to form. It was spring, and I was back at college, this time as a graduate instructor. The summer was going to be free. What better way to spend part of it than chasing ghost crabs on the moonlit Florida sands? The more we thought about it, the more romantic it sounded.

We looked through the list to find what other plants and animals we could collect while there. After all, a couple of hundred ghost crabs weren't going to turn a profit—even at twenty cents apiece. I got several books on the natural history of Florida. Finally we decided on the crop we'd harvest: certain jellyfish, barnacles, molluscs and miscellaneous insects.

I wrote to the biological supply house, offering to get the specimens we'd chosen. "We are glad to learn that you plan to do some collecting this summer," they replied. "Enclosed find our order for the specimens as indicated."

This was simple. We practically had the critters in their jars and the check all spent. All that remained was the mere formality of picking them up like so many ripe plums beneath a tree.

Both of us had kept in touch with friends we'd known in the service. Now we alerted the few who lived in the South, and let them in on the news that they'd be in for a visit from the Roods. Then, just before we actually started, Peg sent them a last-minute card. "Fair warning," it said. "We're really coming."

Finally, many Marine-and-Air-Force reunions later, we found ourselves on the beach. I collected some barnacles around an old hulk, and scouted the sand for signs of ghost crabs. Evidence was there in abundance—odd little pock-marks in double rows over the sand made by their feet, and holes about two inches in diameter into which the crabs retreated during the day.

At dusk the hunt began. Sure enough, as we sneaked close to the spot where I'd seen the greatest number of holes, a shadow moved for a moment and disappeared beneath the sand. Then, as our eyes got used to the dark, we saw another.

"Ps-s-st!" Peg hissed. "Here's one!" She made a dash with the net. "Doggone! Missed him!"

I took off after another, with the same result. Then we both ran at once. Not a crab did we get.

"Whew," said Peg when we were together again. "There's eighty cents we haven't got. Darn 'em—they won't run fair!"

If you've ever tried to chase a crab you know what she meant. If we'd dash left, they'd go right. If we tried to make them run straight ahead, they'd scuttle off to the side. And with four pairs of legs running on tiptoe they were more than a match for a couple of clumsy humans, even if we did have long-handled nets. Peg was right. They just wouldn't run fair.

We kept after them for an hour. By that time we'd become accustomed to the dark. We'd become accustomed to crab ways a bit, too, apparently, for we had eight of the gray-white creatures in a deep box. There they crowded into a corner, watching us, with their fifth pair of legs—the powerful claws—partly raised in defense.

"Well, that's eight crabs," Peg said cheerfully as we counted them. "And in only an hour, too."

Then she peered down more closely. "One of them seems to have lost a claw. Or somebody did. There it is lying on the bottom of the box."

Now we had a new problem. Not only were our crabs hard to get, but they were hard to keep—intact. In Zoology class we'd been told about autotomy, that protective action some creatures have which allows them to shed a body part in an emergency. This orphaned portion, theoretically, keeps an enemy busy while the abbreviated owner can run all the faster. I knew that lizards sometimes shed their tails. Now here was autotomy-while-you-wait in the crustacean world. And, while we waited, a second crabless claw appeared.

This was serious. We had to put the crabs to sleep in a hurry. The supply house wouldn't take them unless they were perfect.

Back to the car I went for the formaldehyde. Peg had caught one more crab and stood holding it in the net, hesitating to put it down into that den of autotomy.

"All right. You're first," I said to the new captive. "Into the formaldehyde with you."

He clung desperately to the net, and fought gamely, but at last I held him up. Peg shone the flashlight on him. We could see the dark, stalked eyes, the leg hairs that kept him from sinking in the sand. Dauntless and undefeated, the plucky little fellow held up his pinchers in defiance.

We admired him silently for a moment. "You know, he's beautiful in a way," Peg said quietly. "Seems almost a shame to kill him."

I glanced at her. Darkness hid her face, but I knew just what her eyes were saying. Mine, I think, were saying the same thing.

"Yes," I said, lowering him to the sand, "we're never going to get enough, anyway. It'll cost us more to run after these fellows for a week than it would just to forget the whole thing." I opened my hand. "Go to it, boy!"

He lost no time in going to it. Just a blurred streak, and our No. 9 crab was gone. Then I tipped the box over and released all the rest.

Well, almost all. I kept the two claws. Their owners, I knew, would grow new weapons in time.

And thus ended the crab concession. But not our vacation or our collecting trip. I popped jellyfish and barnacles into the preservative without a qualm. They hardly seemed like living animals. So we made only about forty dollars less on the trip than we had hoped for.

"Anyway," said Peg later when we figured up our expenses, "we made enough to almost pay for the gasoline."

This first sample of collecting whetted my taste for more. Although I hated to do away with any living thing, I could realize that budding doctors and entomologists had to have their specimens. So I got a book on collecting, and learned how to put insects and other small creatures to sleep painlessly and quickly. Then I wrote to other biological houses and inquired what they needed for their shelves.

It's surprising what some of these places want. Bizarre things like tapeworms and black widow spiders; common things like bumblebees and dragonflies. One firm wanted dog fleas, while another went still further.

"'We could use a thousand body lice at this time,'" Peg read aloud from a listing that had arrived in the mail. "Maybe they could —but *I* couldn't. Don't you *dare* look for a source to fill that order!"

Our biological collecting tours have since helped to defray the cost of many a vacation trip. We would let the dragonflies sparkle in the sun, even though they were on our list, but we had no qualms about putting pestiferous Japanese beetles to sleep for the benefit of some student who'd never seen one. We seldom show much of a profit, but as Peg said at the end of that first trip, "we almost pay for the gasoline."

Now, living on our hundred acres of Vermont countryside, we still pursue our hobby. Jack, our big shepherd dog, did his best not long ago to raise a crop of dog fleas for us after some friends brought their itchy English setter to visit. But Jack's fur was so thick and silky that the fleas got discouraged. So, beyond a reminiscent dig with a hind foot once a day, he has done little to help us make a killing on the flea market.

There are a number of creatures, however, on which we have done well. I noticed that Beauty and Chichi were stamping their hoofs and switching their tails on a summer's day. The horse-flies were nipping them in a dozen places at once. So I let the tormented animals into the barn.

The flies stayed with them for a moment and then flew to the windows. There I picked them off and popped them into a cyanide bottle, where they died almost instantly.

Tom was watching me as I collected the pesky creatures. "How much do you get for each one of those, Dad?"

"Five cents apiece, if they're the right species."

"Golly. You must have a dollar's worth right there. And there must be another buck's worth on the door outside, just waiting for the horses to come out again."

So, all in the interests of science, we led the horses out again. Sure enough, the flies that had been left behind hopped aboard. Then we led the horses back into the barn. And within minutes a second crop of flies had been put to sleep.

We collected botflies off the horses, too. These are creatures that look like a bee, but carry on in a most unbeelike manner. They fly repeatedly at the legs and flanks of the horses in late summer. With each touch to the horse's hair, they deposit a sticky yellow-white egg.

When the horse licks the eggs, they hatch into tiny maggots. Carried on the horse's tongue, they eventually take up residence in its stomach. Here they grow all winter long, sometimes forming a solid patch of uninvited guests on the stomach lining. When

47

summer arrives again, they release their hold, pass out with the droppings of the horse, and turn into new generations of flies.

"Look, Daddy," said Alison one day as we were saddling the horses. "All those botfly eggs on Beauty's legs. They can't all hatch out and get into her stomach, can they? She wouldn't have room for any grass."

I bent down and examined our faithful old mare. She had thousands of the little nits on her forelegs and lower body. It looked as if someone had sprinkled her with yellow sugar. Then we thought over the long journey they had to travel from one generation to another, and realized that a great majority of the eggs would be doomed to failure. Many would not be licked by Beauty's warm, moist tongue and hence would remain on her legs unhatched. Others would not transfer successfully to her mouth. And those that did make it might be left abandoned in her droppings when she changed pastures, or be deposited far from home when we were riding her. Hence thousands of eggs were needed to produce mere dozens of adult botflies.

This is the way with many parasites, our county agent assured me when I asked him about them. "You look in a ditch at the edge of your pasture sometime in summer," he said, "and you may find swarms of horsefly larvae—thousands of 'em. But actually only a very few adults will ever successfully find another horse."

We did our own share, on occasion, toward the care and feeding of parasites. "There's a firm out in Chicago that wants a thousand blackflies," I told Peg one spring day. "Care to help me collect them?"

"You mean those little humpbacked gnats that bit like fire the last time we visited the beaver pond? No thanks."

But in the end she came along. And so we spent a memorable evening, watching beavers at the pond, putting blackfiies in bottles of alcohol—and swatting—until we could stand it no longer. But we were several hundred short of our goal. However, as we got back to the car, we realized that swarms of them were coming right along with us. Then we remembered the cue from the horses in the barn. We took our little friends into the car, rolled up the windows—and picked them right off the glass.

In a few minutes that part of Vermont was freed of a thousand blackflies. In spite of my loyalty to my adopted state, though, I can't say that it did much to improve conditions. A spring night along a tumbling stream in the Green Mountain State is still, shall we say, rarely spent alone. You'll usually have lots of company.

Of course, it's important to be able to identify positively the specimens you're collecting. One kind may be in great demand, while another which resembles it may be worthless. This explains, perhaps, why there aren't more collectors in the business. It also explains why I let a small bonanza slip through my hands.

This happened while I was spending an August vacation on Long Island. Rumor had it that the bluefish were running in the surf, so I packed my gear and went after them.

But the rumor must have been started by some tackle store, for I was soon joined by crowds of fishermen, many with the latest rigs and lures just bought for the occasion. Yet before long it was apparent that the only bluefish around were in Ray's Market on the edge of town.

There had been a storm a day or two before, and the beach was littered with debris. The waves were still running high. After losing a lure on a piece of floating wreckage and tangling another one up for ten minutes, I decided to try a sheltered inlet where the water would be calm.

As I cast my hook into the water I noticed something floating in front of me. Then I saw another, and another. The water was alive with hundreds and thousands of jellyfish of a kind that I didn't immediately recognize.

"Must have been blown in from the open ocean by the storm," I thought, and went on fishing.

When the bluefish still refused to show themselves, I took another

49

glance at the jellyfish. "Wonder if they're worth anything as specimens?" I asked myself. "Better take a few along—just in case."

So I scooped a few dozen into a bucket of preservative and went home.

"Did you have any luck?" Peg asked.

"None. Well, nothing but a few jellyfish."

I forgot the specimens for a day or two. Then I pulled out a guide-book to identify them. Sure enough, they were a kind I had never collected before. I checked the catalogues of the supply houses; none of them listed this species for sale.

Packing up individual specimens, I sent a sample to each of the firms I'd supplied in the past. Every one of them answered:

"Yes, we are interested. Please tell us how many you can supply."

"We would like to include a thousand of these in our listings."

"We have not listed this type for several years, and would be interested in obtaining a supply for our new catalogue."

I rushed back to the beach. The jellyfish were nowhere to be seen. With sinking heart, I typed out my reply.

"Thank you for your interest. However, I regret to inform you that I cannot supply the jellyfish at this time."

I sent this letter off to all the firms but one. To this firm I sent my few dozen jellyfish. Back came their check. I figured out the rate of pay on this particular deal. It was slightly more than fifty dollars an hour. And I'd muffed my chance.

So, as I say, you have to be able to identify positively the specimens you're collecting. And you have to do it at the right time.

By the way, the bluefish were biting on the occasion of my second visit to the beach. But of course I didn't have my fishing tackle with me then.

Perhaps the strangest order I've yet filled was for five hundred sea urchins. These prickly first cousins to the starfish are a mass of spines, which makes them about as hospitable as an underwater porcupine. One kind, I'm told, even swings its spines around so they all point toward an intruder.

CHASING GHOSTS

The sea urchins we needed to collect could be found just a foot or two beneath low-tide mark on the Maine coast. This sounded simple enough to us: just wait for low tide, wade out, and pick up five hundred urchins. But there were a couple of hitches that we didn't fully realize until a little later.

Armed with the order for the urchins, Peg and I set aside a weekend. Friday noon we started out for the Maine coast with a couple of friends. My books had told me the urchins would be found on what the Down Easters call "ha'd bottom"—rocks and ledges. So we headed for a rocky chunk of shoreline I'd once visited in the neighborhood of Frenchman's Bay.

When we got there around supper time, our first complication was waiting for us. "What time's low tide?" I asked the caretaker at the campground where we stayed.

"Four o'clock."

"You mean four o'clock tomorrow morning? While it's still dark?"

"Yep. But don't you worry none. There'll be another one 'bout four-thirty tomorrow afternoon."

"But we came all the way from Vermont! And the trip's no good unless we get all the low tides we can!"

"Well, now, I'll tell you. You go out tomorrow morning about four o'clock and there'll be one right there on the beach."

I glanced at Peg. She was giving me her Look. It says anything and everything. This time it plainly spoke: "You *know* that the tide is a different time every day. And so why didn't you check on the tides before we chose *this* weekend?"

As it was, we had a full day to quiz around and find just where the best sea-urchin territory might be. We rented a boat and loaded all our gear into it, ready for the turn of the tide.

Then the second complication crept in. Perhaps I should say it swept out. For the tides in that part of Maine may be thirty feet or more in height. When you have hundreds of square miles of sea changing in level some thirty feet, you've got a tremendous flow of water. So "low tide" was a point in time and little more. The instant the water hit low mark, it turned and started up again.

For half an hour before and half an hour after low tide we worked feverishly, picking the underwater cactus-critters off the rocks. We hung on to the sides of the rowboat and put our prey in the bottom. Finally the rowboat was lifted so high by the rising water that each urchin began to represent a skin-diving expedition. Panting, we climbed aboard and peered down at the hundreds of urchins that still clung to the rocks. Our fingers and toes were sore from the spines, and we were chilled from the Maine water.

"Boy," grumbled one of our companions, "I've heard of friendship. But since when does friendship include getting waterlogged, speared, and dying from exposure?"

Nevertheless, there we were at the next low tide in the cold dawn. More splinters, more chills—and the five hundred urchins were ours.

Back to shore we rowed our prizes. We were met at the dock by the gentleman who owned the boat.

He looked in disbelief at our catch. "'Sea urchins,' you call them? Why, we call 'em porcupine eggs. And who'd ever want to bring in a boatload of porcupine eggs?"

We were too exhausted to argue. Packing our urchins into pails and boxes, we piled into the car. But just before I started the motor, I heard him speak to another man who had watched the whole procedure in silence:

"Folks from Vermont. Can't figure out what they're doing. Chasing ghosts, if you ask me."

Which may be just about right.

Tent caterpillars (by Larry Pringle for National Audubon Society) and, *right*, garter snake with young (American Museum of Natural History).

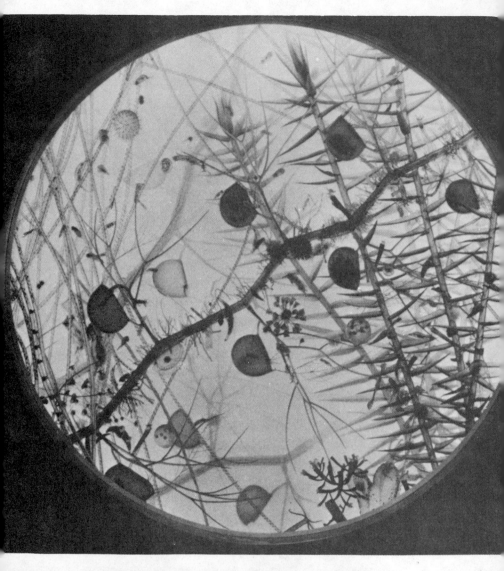

Pond life magn[...]
1,000,000 times, pai[...]
turtle and, *opp*[...]
ghost crab (all [...]
American Museu[...]
Natural History).

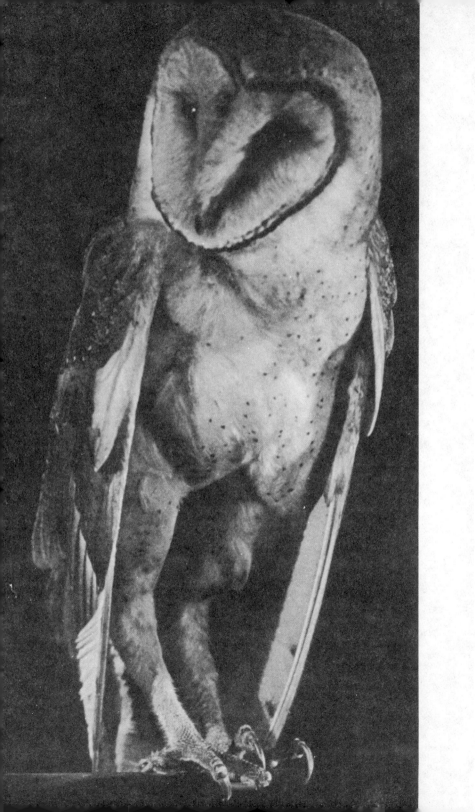

Tyto alba, here wide awake, *left;* vantage point for a raccoon (both American Museum of Natural History), and black widow with her egg sac (by Grace A. Thompson for National Audubon Society).

Audubon's famous portrait of loons (American Museum of Natural History). Ed Morgan, *right*, with my bathtub boarder, and frogs back in hibernation in the refrigerator.

Nature's protection for a fawn in our woods.

Three stages of ducklings hatching in an electric fry-pan at a constant 102° (photographed by Chet Callahan).

CHAPTER SIX

Drowsy 'Chucks, Sleepy Monkeys, and Lady Macbeth

WHEN I RECEIVED an advanced degree from the University of Connecticut a year after my ghost-crab days, my position as a graduate instructor terminated. At the same time came the offer of a position at the Long Island Agricultural and Technical Institute.

I accepted the offer. Now I'd be able to fish and roam the beaches as much as I wished. Perhaps I'd have the chance to collect those rare jellyfish if I was right on the spot. Or at any rate, I could carry on my other type of "collecting"—storing away facts about the creatures that I would find living there.

The beach would be fine for the children, too. Janice was just kindergarten age. Tom was two years behind her. Alison, our next-to-youngest, was expected at any moment. In fact, when Peg had got her bachelor's degree the same time I got my master's, she had been obviously pregnant. Even the loose graduation gown hadn't been able to hide that fact. So you can imagine the delighted howl that went up from the audience as President Jorgensen presented her with her diploma, saying pointedly into the microphone:

"Margaret B. Rood—majoring in *Child Development!*"

Now our growing family found a little ranch home in Massapequa. Its "ranch" consisted of a plot of struggling lawn about eighty feet square. On three sides were other ranches. But although I had no broad acreage of my own, I found plenty of room to wander at nearby Tackapausha Park and the grounds of the Long Island Institute.

My duties were to teach Biology and a course in plant protection. I tried to instill in my students the idea of living with plants and animals to learn about them. We took frequent walks through the gardens and pastures of the Institute and watched living things in their natural surroundings. We might take a salamander or frog back to the laboratory, but always we let it go again in a day or so.

There were other people on Long Island who were learning to live with animals and plants, too. Long Island's mushrooming suburban growth in the early 1950's led thousands of people into contact with a semblance of the wide open spaces—many of them for the first time. They turned to the Institute for information. And so my natural interest led me to try to help with some of their questions. These ranged all the way from how to care for a sick rosebush to what to do for termites in a honeymoon cottage.

Some of these requests came in the form of boxes and packages in the morning's mail. Others came as worried homemakers or their spouses, patiently sitting in the outer office with a bundle of something-or-other that whispered or scratched or occasionally moved as they waited. Still other requests arrived by telephone. Sometimes we could make suggestions immediately, but often we had to ferret out all the facts before we made a diagnosis:

"My elm looks all brown, Mr. Rood. What can I do to save it?"
"Well, it's impossible to say over the phone without further information. Does it get plenty of water?"

"Oh, yes. It gets as much water as the other elms, and they're all nice and green."

"Has there been any digging, or road-building, or other work that would damage the roots?"

"No, this is in our back yard. And the street's out front."

"And you say your other elms are all healthy. Do you see any evidence of insect attack on the foliage?"

"Insects? I should say not! How could they live with the incinerator right beneath the tree?"

We told her it'd help a lot to move her incinerator.

Dr. Lou Pyenson, the head of the Biology department, had as much fun answering these questions as I did. One of the hardest to answer was what we called the "loose-leaf letter," which consisted of a single leaf or two from a tree or shrub, along with questions as to what was wrong, what would make it right, and what was the plant anyway? Sometimes we could identify the plant, spot the disease and prescribe a cure, all in a sentence or two. This would be easy if it was a maple leaf, say, covered with insect galls, or a birch leaf tunneled with leaf-miners. These two are cared for with the proper insecticide at the right time.

Other times, though, it'd be two or three unhappy hunks of greenery torn from somebody's shrub. Then you had to guess the rest: whether it had just been transplanted from a nursery, whether it was being bumped almost daily by a power mower, whether the neighbor's dog visited it twice a day, and so on.

In such cases you usually ended up writing the homeowner for more information or suggesting that he see his local nurseryman to save time. Still, since it's only human to put off things as long as possible, we often suspected that the poor thing had been gasping with its last lenticel before we were even thought of in the first place.

Of course many people brought their problems in to us directly. The farmer in the country with row upon row of plants or with great rolling fields could rely on his local county agricultural extension agent. Many of the brand-new householders who came to us for advice, however, were for the first time in their lives the owners of a few square feet of land. So they knew nothing of county agents or how to grow plants. To them the loss of a single shrub was a personal tragedy. Hence they would arrive with a sprig of yellowbell or a clump of browned grass, sitting in the outer office like a small boy with a sick puppy. And when we finally had the chance to talk with them, it did no good to tell them that one bush in twenty could be expected to die at transplanting. This *was* the one bush—the only bush—they had.

Yet we clucked sympathetically with many a visitor over a listless lilac or a homesick willow and wished there were some way to take a plant's pulse or stick a thermometer in a tree.

The Bringers of Animals were the most interesting of all. Usually, I must admit, they got first attention if at all possible. This was often the case if their bundle, box or bag squealed, squirmed or—occasionally—smelled. And it became almost a rule after Mr. Coates brought in the woodchuck.

I confess that we kept him waiting longer than we should have. A sweet young thing from Bayshore and her husband had purchased an unimproved lot on a stretch of beach. They wished to build a cottage in the spring, and wondered which plants to cut down and which to leave for future use. So she brought in a number of twigs from the shrubs in question. "Which of these are worth saving?" she asked.

She was so obviously a damsel in distress that we gallantly came to the rescue. She was a pretty one, too, and we took our time about it.

Nobody was in the waiting room when we first started on the identification of the twigs. Mr. Coates must have walked in quietly and taken his place, waiting his turn. It was some time before I happened to glance out and see him sitting there.

He clutched a large burlap bag. It, too, had a sense of urgency.

So I called him in to a side room.

"It's a woodchuck," he said, carefully opening the top of the bag. "I don't know what to do with him. I live in an old house that we're hitching a garage to. The contractors uncovered him when they were doing some bulldozing. He must have been hibernating under an old rubbish pile. I can't let him go now, in February. Do you people want him?"

I shrugged helplessly. "Well, actually, we're not . . ."

But I never got any further. Mr. Coates's bag suddenly lifted in the air as the weight went out of it. What looked like about eight pounds of grizzled-red rodent scooted across the floor and out the door before either of us could move.

"Well, whaddya know?" Mr. Coates murmured. "He must have chewed his way out through the bag while I was waiting in the other room. The bag was okay when I took it out of the car."

I stood there, mouth open. Then I snatched the bag from him. Then I thrust it back as I reached for a wastebasket by the desk. "Here. You take the bag. I'm going to see if I can put the wastebasket over him."

Out the door we went. There were seven or eight doors opening on the hall. He could have gone into any of them—any but one, that is. This one opened into the suite of offices where the twig identification work was still going on. The low sound of voices assured me that, at least, the woodchuck wasn't in there. Closing this door carefully, I was just about to say something when Mr. Coates spoke in a low voice.

"There he is. At the head of the stairs."

"Oh, no! If he ever gets downstairs we'll lose him in all the classrooms!"

We stood our ground, hoping the 'chuck would change his mind. He remained poised on the landing. Slowly I turned my head until I could see a clock. I had seven minutes before the bell rang for change of classes. And still the woodchuck paused, deciding which course to take.

Then, slowly, without the least hint of hurry, he began to descend the stairs one at a time.

"Should we rush him?" Mr. Coates asked.

"No. Let's wait 'til he's reached bottom and then see where he goes."

I prayed that the lack of classroom sounds from below meant the doors were shut. I could just see the result if an ex-hibernating woodchuck chanced into any one of these rooms with a couple of dozen boys and girls. I didn't care about the psychological effect so much as I worried about those strong white chisel-teeth: they could slice a finger to the bone or rip through shoe leather. A cornered woodchuck is a terrible adversary, and I figured one rooted out of bed by a bulldozer would be ten times as bad.

With every step the woodchuck took downward, we took a step forward. Finally he had reached the floor of the downstairs hall. There he began to snoop along the edge of the wall, sniffing at each door as we slowly descended the stairs. There were several empty rooms at the end of the hall. Perhaps he'd go into one of them. Then, at least, we'd have him confined in a small place.

He paused at the entrance to the first room. "Go on in there," I heard Mr. Coates plead under his breath. But again our 'chuck paused. He sniffed and looked, sat up and scratched. He lowered himself and sniffed again. And then the bell rang.

Almost instantly several classroom doors burst open. Down the hall went the woodchuck, and we lost him behind a wall of milling students.

"*Now* where is he?" groaned my companion.

I looked at poor Mr. Coates. He was mortified at the trouble his 'chuck was causing. It wasn't his fault we'd kept him waiting. Probably he had to get back to work. "Tell you what," I said, "why not just help me get every door closed as quickly as we can. I'm sure he's in one of those empty classrooms. Then we'll put some signs up not to open them. You can go back to work or wherever you're going, and I've got half a dozen students who'll have the time of their lives catching him after school."

He looked immensely relieved, and we closed the doors. "Thanks a lot," I grinned at him as he headed for the front entrance. "And if you run into any skunks . . ."

"I know," he said: "forget 'em. Well, I sure am sorry. Good luck in your woodchuck hunt."

During the next few minutes I strolled into each downstairs classroom. Nodding pleasantly at the instructor, I wandered nonchalantly around until I had assured myself that there weren't any woodchucks there. Finally, when I had the rooms all checked, I put warning signs up on the closed doors and waited for the day to finish.

After school we called for student volunteers. "Now, you take this wastebasket," I said, showing them how to feint and parry with it like a lion-tamer with a chair. "Old 'Chuck is probably plenty grumpy, so you've got to watch him. And he's surprisingly strong. So if you find him, clamp the basket down on top of him. Then sit on it and don't move until somebody comes."

We opened the classroom doors cautiously and went inside, two to a room. Nothing in our room. Carefully stepping outside, I stood in the hall and waited for a commotion. But one by one the doors opened again until all of us were assembled once more. No woodchuck.

"But he's got to be there," I insisted. "He's got to be in *some* room."

Whether he had to be or not, he wasn't. We checked every corner of every room thoroughly. We even looked in the desks and chairs.

Finally there was nothing to do but call off the search. I left a note for the janitor to call me if he found the 'chuck. Then I went home shaking my head. Perhaps I'd dreamed it. After all, the only other person to see it had been Mr. Coates—and I had forgotten to get his address.

When classes began in the morning I waited for the summons that I felt sure would come. Any moment I expected to be called to rescue a terrorized class or—horrors—take some student to the doctor with a ferocious woodchuck bite. But not a shred of evidence as to my 'chuck's whereabouts was there all day. Perhaps he had gotten away somehow. Yet I felt sure he was still in the building.

By late afternoon my nerves had finally dulled, and I forgot the woodchuck. Therefore I was completely unprepared when the news finally came.

"Mr. Rood," said a student from the doorway of my office, "your woodchuck's in the building."

"That's nice."

"No. No fooling. In the drafting room."

"*What?*"

"In the drafting room. In the bookcase. Right where we all looked last night."

"Good heavens. Is the door shut?" I asked as we hastened down the stairs.

"Oh, there's no need of that. He won't get away. Wait'll you see him."

There was, indeed, no necessity to close the door. In my anxiety over the woodchuck, I had forgotten two basic things about his personality.

First, he is in reality a large ground-squirrel. We'd been looking for him mostly around the floor and on the chairs, giving little thought to anything more than waist-high. Yet I've seen woodchucks in trees more than once, like their striped ground-dwelling cousins, the little chipmunks. Therefore a bookcase presented no problem to him.

Second, his nap had been interrupted. The temperature of the bookshelf, built against the cool wall of the building, must have approximated the temperature of the cozy den he'd left behind. So, finding a spot at the end of a row of books, he'd curled up in a ball, looking half like a clump of books himself.

And there he was now, sound asleep.

Gently we eased a thin board under him and took him down cellar. There he stayed until the weather began to slacken. Then we took him further out on Long Island and released him. Perhaps even today he munches his clover and reminisces about the time he went to college.

Since woodchucks are prime targets for boys with guns in the countryside because of real and fancied damage to crops and hayland, we were often asked as to the way to raise an orphan 'chuck. Mammals that they are, they do well on milk sweetened a bit with honey; after they're about six weeks old they'll switch to greenery such as clover, weeds and grass. They make interesting little pets when small, but show few sparks of genius when grown. They're apt to become snappish, too. One pet 'chuck I knew of terrorized the whole family one afternoon until they managed to throw a blanket over it and capture it.

Another question we often got was how to keep woodchucks from going where they weren't wanted. We've not found a good answer yet. Low electric fences are sometimes effective, but they're costly. So are mothballs spread around as a repellent. Poisons thrown into their tunnels have a certain degree of danger to other animals.

Still, woodchucks aren't all bad. Their holes may be used as shelter by other animals. And one of the eight-pound rodents sitting upright in a meadow adds something to the scene.

Drowsy woodchucks weren't our only problem. One afternoon the phone rang in the secretary's office. "Somebody's probably got a sick sycamore," Lou Pyenson grinned as we could hear Marie taking down an address.

"All right," we heard her say in her best don't-call-us-we'll-call-you voice. "We're certainly interested to know about it. And if one of our people is free, he'll be over as soon as possible—consistent with a heavy teaching schedule, of course. In the meantime, thank you for calling."

Harvey Barke had been listening in an adjacent office. " 'Sick sycamore' my eye," he chuckled. Then he whistled appreciatively at Marie's telephone strategy. "Sounds more like a dead dog-wood—probably the bark's all gone."

"Very funny," called Doc from his desk. "Almost as funny as when you made the same crack two days ago . . ."

"Yesterday," corrected Harvey.

"Yesterday. But anyway, Marie, what is it that we're supposed to go take a look at some summer if we're not on vacation?"

In answer she appeared at the door of the Pyenson-Rood office. "A sleepy monkey," she announced.

"A *what*?"

"A sleepy monkey. At least that's what they think they have found. It's some contractor 'way down past Islip. He's tearing down an old shed so he can put up a housing development. And there's a monkey that must have escaped from a zoo somewhere. Or maybe he's somebody's pet. But he sits on one of the beams in the shed and they wonder if we were interested to look at him before the Humane Society takes him away. I took the address, but it sounds like it's an hour's drive from here."

Hour's drive or not, the idea of a monkey on the loose intrigued us. "Ron, that's sort of on your way home," Doc said. "I'm as curious as you probably are. Why not start home a little early and take a look at it?"

So awhile later I pulled alongside a little shack that bore a hand-lettered sign: COMPANY OFFICE.

"You the fella from the Instatoot?" a gentleman in a hard hat asked.

I nodded.

"Well, he's still there. Humane Society ain't been here yet. They're trying to find a big ladder, I guess. But I wish somebody'd come get him. Or at least tell us just exactly how to get rid of him. My men are afraid to take the shed apart any further for fear they'll get bit."

We started off toward the old shed which, half demolished,

stood at the edge of a field. I asked him what they meant when they said he was "sleepy."

"Just sets there. Or maybe he's hurt. One of the men thinks he may have been hit when a two-by-four fell down this noon. But we're taking no chances. He looks sick to me. Maybe he's got rabbits or something."

We strode to the end of the shed, followed by a flying wedge of workmen. At the doorway we came to a halt. I had brought a net and a stout burlap sack, although I had little idea of using either. Now I busied myself with them, ostensibly waiting for my eyes to get used to the gloom, but really considering my chances with a net against a nimble monkey—especially if he happened to be mad with a case of "rabbits."

"Right up there," the foreman indicated. "He's at the other end from here. About seventy-five feet away."

The crowd around us fell silent. Straining my eyes, I advanced, net at the ready. Hard as I looked, I could not see a thing.

"Flashlight," I murmured, like a surgeon asking for a scalpel. "Anybody got a flashlight?"

At the sound of my voice two things happened. The first was three loud snaps—like a pencil slapped on a book in rapid succession. The second was a muffled crash in the corner of the shed.

Then a third thing happened. Silence. This was worse than the other two. I'm not normally greatly afraid of animals, but to face an unknown monkey in the dark when you're a good silhouette against the doorway . . .

"Jeest!" I heard the foreman yell from outside the shed. "None of you guys got a flashlight yet?" I was about to run out and help look for a flashlight somewhere in the next county when some helpful individual came forward.

"Here's one. Ralph had it in his car."

The foreman came into the shed, shining the light before him. "What was that crash? Think he jumped down?"

For answer, I took the light and shone it in the corner of the shed. And there was my monkey.

Two large eyes in a heart-shaped face stared at me from above a huddled body. One "arm" was tucked in close, while the other hung down, drooping.

"What the devil is that?" breathed the foreman. "That ain't no monkey. It looks more like a hawk. Or an owl."

And owl it was—one of the finest mousetraps produced by nature—the monkey-faced, or barn, owl. The off-balance wing showed the reason it had crashed to the floor when it tried to fly. It must have been injured when the building was being torn down. I gave the flashlight to the foreman. "You just shine the light right in his eyes," I said. "I'll see if I can pop the net over on top of him."

Sneaking up, I lowered the net down as gently as I could, for I didn't want to hurt his wing any further. At once we heard the snapping sounds again. Now we could see their source—the powerful beak that gnashed and clicked in rage as he thrashed for a moment in his prison.

Once inside the bag, however, he quickly quieted down. I allowed the men a peek at him when we got out into the open again. "Boy, he sure's got a face like a monkey," said one. "You could have fooled me."

We admired the white breast, the buffy-brown back. His wing didn't seem broken; only twisted. "What are you going to do with him?" asked the foreman.

"Don't you fellows want to nurse him back to health?"

"Naw. He'd be a big deal for about a day. Then we'd be calling you up to come get him. Besides, we wouldn't know how to care for him. What do they eat, anyway?"

I'd read somewhere that a barn owl was worth a dozen hungry cats as far as mice were concerned, for he could swoop on the mice out of the air. "Well, they eat mice and rats. But I'll have to see if he'll take hamburg or stew meat. At least 'til his wing heals. Then he can go catch his own mice again."

So it was that Titus—our version of *Tyto alba*, his scientific name—came to live at "The Institoot" for a few weeks. The students took to him at once. They solved my meat problem in a jiffy, too. The local town dump was overrun with rats and the boys soon had a one-rat-a-day delivery service going.

Titus more than repaid us for our attentions. For the first few days he carried on in fine style—snapping his beak and hissing with a long-drawn-out siss "like my car radiator boiling over," as one student put it. Yet Titus was astonishingly gentle. When I reached in with heavily gloved hands to bandage the hurt wing, he quieted down and allowed me to touch him. Philosopher that he turned out to be, he even wore the white bandage with profound dignity.

The students never tired of contemplating those four claws—two front and two rear on each foot—that reached out with such accuracy when he was presented with a mouse. They watched in fascination as he solemnly blinked one eye, or both, with lids that were almost human. And they burst out laughing when first they saw him turn his head—apparently completely around so he could see directly behind him.

I took Titus's bandage off after about ten days. Daily he exercised his wings—rising on his toes and flapping until his eighteen-inch body was lifted clear off the floor. Finally, about a month after we'd first put him in his cage, we knew it was time to give him his freedom.

Half the school turned out to see him go. I waited until a Friday evening so I'd have the weekend to get him again, if necessary. After supper several of the students carried the big cage out to the front lawn. Then I carefully opened the door. Reaching in, I placed my hand under Titus's claws. Obligingly he mounted my wrist. Lifting him out of the cage, I admired him for the last time. "Okay, Titus. See you around."

He turned that swivel-neck in first one direction and then the other. Crouching ever so slightly, he paused just a minute. Then suddenly the weight was gone from my wrist. Away went our barn owl, silently, surely, like a great quiet big-headed moth in the twilight.

We watched him until we could see him no more. Then I turned to the cage. It seemed so empty, so impossible that it had ever held an owl. "Gee," said one student, "he's gone."

"Yeah," said another. "But aren't owls wonderful birds, when you get to know them?"

I knew then that Titus had done his job well. He'd taught my boys and girls better than I could have done it myself. For, as a naturalist, I long had known what they'd just put into words: that everything wild is wonderful, once you get to know it.

One of the students who was most sorry to see Titus go was a girl named Ruth. She had been a constant helper during the time we had him. She cleaned his cage, saw to it that he was fed at the proper time, and showed him to visitors.

In fact, Ruth was one of my favorite students. Somehow in her education she'd escaped the unfortunate deadening of interest and initiative which so often sets in at about eighth grade. The world was still new and exciting to her, even though she'd graduated from high school. Now, at nineteen, she was back in school —this time at the Agricultural Institute for further training.

Give her a microscope and a piece of a leaf and she'd soon be as absorbed as a child with a jigsaw puzzle. Where the other students would squirm as they took the innards out of a preserved frog, Ruthie would be going for all she was worth. "Look," she'd say to Charlie, who was her laboratory partner and boyfriend, "here's the frog's tongue. And see how funny it's hitched—at the front, so he can flip it out at bugs and things. And here's his stomach. I bet if we opened him up, we could find out exactly what he ate."

Then, like as not, she'd follow her own suggestion, carefully spreading the frog's last meal on a piece of white paper after other students had been only too glad to pack up and get out when the period ended.

My fellow teachers said she was like this in all her classes. And once when I talked on natural history to a group of fifth-graders, I saw a whole roomful of Ruths. A forest of hands would fly up every time I'd ask a question. Even if they didn't have the answer, they'd at least give it a try.

Sometimes, when I peer down into a flower or gaze through a lens at the marvel of developing frog eggs, I feel some of the same thrill that Ruth and those fifth-graders must have had. Then I can understand Mr. Lake's comment as he brought me home years ago from an arrowhead expedition:

"As a naturalist, Ronald, I see everything through the eyes of a child."

I like to think that some of that enthusiasm he displayed was handed through me to Ruth. Perhaps I merely encouraged her natural curiosity as Mr. Lake had once done for me. At any rate, her zest for life was boundless.

Poor Charlie was caught in the middle of it. His affection for Ruth wasn't necessarily supposed to include a liking for frogs' dinners and related things, but it ended up doing nearly just that. On our field trips she'd load him with guidebooks and knapsacks while she carried camera and binoculars. But this was all fine with Charlie. He worshiped the very ground she trod—even if he had to tote a portable laboratory over every inch of it.

When Christmas vacation came that year, Ruth met me the day before with glowing eyes. "Mr. Rood, you'll never guess. I'm going to Florida with my folks for Christmas. What do you want me to bring back?"

I thought for a while. "How about a little palm tree?" I asked. "This is something that's typically Florida. But just a tiny one."

She agreed to the palm tree, plus "anything else I can find."

At once I thought of alligators. Or—who could tell?—Ruth

might even bring home a tarpon. "Well," I hastened to say, "if you find some other *little* thing, that's fine."

Sure enough, after vacation Ruth brought me a palm tree, one she'd dug up herself to guarantee its being a genuine Florida product. Then she reached into a paper bag she was carrying and produced a small cardboard box punched with holes.

"This was native, too. I found it under the boards of a lumber pile."

She handed it to me. Written on it was DANGER! OPEN WITH CARE. I hesitated. "Will it jump out at me?" I asked.

"Oh, no. It's right at home in its box. Just don't stick your finger down in there, that's all. At least, not from what I've read about it." Obviously she enjoyed keeping its identity a mystery.

Just the same, after eyeing the jungle of chairs and desks in the classroom, I decided to open it in the lab where it couldn't get away.

Slowly I removed the lid. Ruth was right. The denizen of the box was right at home—she and her two hundred babies. Beady-black and shiny, she hung motionless and upside down in her web, the orange hourglass-marking unmistakable on her underside.

"Black widow spider," volunteered Ruth. "You said to get something little, so here she is. And all her babies, too. Hatched a few days ago."

Well, now. This was almost beyond the call of duty. "What'd your folks say when you told them you were bringing me one of America's most fearsome creatures?" I asked.

She looked sheepish. "To tell the truth, I put it in my suitcase so they wouldn't know about it."

Definitely beyond the call of duty. Right there I resolved that Ruth would pass Biology even if, somehow, she flunked the rest of the course. I didn't dare have her another year: there are rattlesnakes in Florida, too.

I bent down to look at the babies. They were thin, long-legged, tan and white, nothing like their round-bodied mother. The whitish egg sac in which they'd been hatched was tucked in one corner of the box. The sac had been found under the boards and put in with the mother, who'd woven it right into her new web.

Obviously our first job was to find a suitable container for such a lethal family. We finally decided on a terrarium with a tight-fitting glass cover. Then I looked up all the material I could find on Black Widows, Care and Feeding of.

She was frightening indeed, according to the books. Drop for drop, her venom was more poisonous than that of a rattlesnake. Nevertheless, the experts said, there were several redeeming factors. Black widows have just a tiny bit of venom. They're very secretive and prefer to hide in out-of-the-way places. And, most important, they'd just as soon not bite. This was evident from the fact that, although they've been found in every state of the Union, there are only about half a hundred recorded deaths from their bite in some fifteen hundred known cases.

"What do I feed the babies?" Ruth asked. "The book says they eat aphids and other little insects. But where do you find insects this time of the year?"

I sent her over to the Institute's greenhouse. She and Charlie returned with a sprig of curled-up leaves, covered with aphids. They also had a couple of flies in a bottle. "Flies for mother, aphids for the children," she said.

We put the insects out in the cold to numb them for easy handling. Then we went to shake them into the web.

Ruth lifted the glass cover carefully. "Good heavens!" she exclaimed. "Where did they all go?"

I looked down at the two hundred spiders. Only there weren't two hundred. There were just about half that number.

For a moment I had visions of a hundred spiderlings all over the lab. Then, looking closer, we understood. The remaining babies had begun to grow up overnight. Where they'd been slender and delicate before, they now had a certain roundness. We'd been too slow with the aphids, and the spiders had tackled each other.

We decided they had to be separated, so Ruth and Charlie

carefully transferred the spiderlings to pint bottles, about ten per bottle. There they made little webs of their own. The two students heroically kept them supplied with aphids, but the family squabbles continued.

In two months they were down to just a dozen spiders. At first they had all looked alike, but now the males could be distinguished from the females. Harlequin striped, with gay colors and banded legs, they were less than half the size of their sisters, whose juvenile stripes were rapidly giving over to jet black on their raisin-sized bodies. Every time the spiders shed their skins in growth, the differences in size and color became more apparent.

Mother black widow hadn't survived more than a couple of weeks after we put her in the terrarium. However, because all my students had now become interested in the fate of her dwindling brood of orphans, we decided to try to start a new family.

We checked our books as to how to play Cupid. The books weren't very helpful. "The black widow," said one, "is so named because she is apt to feed on her mate." Another book approached the subject with more delicacy. "Males and females are seldom found in the same web," it stated chastely, leaving the reader about where he'd been in the first place. So we put the books away and started off on our own.

We began by putting two of the males in a jar with the largest female. The trial was an instant success—from her standpoint, that is. Black widows capture their prey by lassoing them with globs of silk from their abdomen, using their hind feet to pull it out in a sticky skein. And in about the time it takes to tell of it here, both males were globbed and skeined. Then she punctured each with those lethal fangs and proceeded to dine at her leisure.

We watched woefully as the big female cut short our hopes. "Looks as if the way to a black widow's heart is not through her stomach," observed Charlie.

"That's a thought," Ruth said. "Maybe she was too hungry for romance. Why not feed her within an inch of her life and try it again?"

'CHUCKS, MONKEYS, AND LADY MACBETH

We'd been feeding at the rate of a single fly a day; now we doubled the rations. Finally, after our little Lady Macbeth had been stuffed for a week, we decided the time was right for another trial.

"Here, Lady," Ruth coaxed, "here's a nice handsome boyfriend for you." With that, she carefully put a single male in the jar and closed the lid.

For half a minute nothing happened. This, in itself, was a hopeful sign. Then the gentleman spider began to take courage. Carefully, cautiously, he twitched the web. Still no sign of hospitality.

More twitchings, more waitings. Then, almost miraculously, Lady began to give in. Once, twice, three times she twitched the web right back.

From here things worked up to the height of passion, black-widow style. Twitch answered twitch until finally the little male had made his way to the side of his partner. She seemed huge by comparison.

"Look what he's doing now," Ruthie spoke in an awed voice. "He's catching *her* in a web."

As we watched, the male pulled delicate strands of silk from his body and cast them about his lady love. Obviously they were just token bonds, for she could easily have pulled free of them. Then began the process of mating.

There was no actual genital contact between the two. Like many spiders, the male carried his sperm in special bulbous palps, or leglike feelers. They looked like big antennae near the front of his head. Having deposited the sperm earlier on a sheet of web, he had stored it in the palps. Now he placed it in her reproductive opening, up at the forward end of her abdomen. Then he stood by while she broke free of her shroud.

"And, so," quoted Ruth, "they were married. But will they live happily ever after?"

We decided to leave Lucky, as we dubbed him, right in the same jar with his mate. To increase his chances of survival, we kept the double-ration system in effect. Possibly the necessity of having to live so close to his spouse kept his appetite down, however, for we never saw him take any food from that day on. In a few weeks we found him at the bottom of the jar, apparently dead from starvation.

Lady's appetite, however, was dulled by no sense of mourning. She consumed each fly, catching it with marvelous skill. She'd approach it in the web, then turn about quickly, throwing a bolo of sticky silk at it from a tail-first position. Hauling out strands of the stuff with those hind legs in alternation, she'd fling it around with surprising accuracy as she backed toward her victim. Then, pulling out more web, she would turn the fly over and over with her hind legs until it was encased completely in a white shroud.

Now, seemingly for the first time, she'd cast her eyes on her victim. Picking out just the right spot for a bite, she'd approach with those deadly fangs. A small dose of venom, and in a few minutes all would be still.

Ruth sometimes watched Lady through a magnifying glass as the spider consumed her meal. "Did you realize," she asked me one day, "that spiders do more than just poison their victims with venom? I've read about it, and now you can see it happening."

Taking the magnifier, I could see that Lady's latest meal was losing shape. She had injected a digestive juice out through her fangs; as it dissolved the tissues from within, they became semi-liquid. When she cut the fly loose after working it over thoroughly, it was little more than a tangled mass of indigestible wings and legs.

Ruth also looked up the effect of black-widow venom on humans, and found that people had been operated on for appendicitis after being bitten by the spider. Although little more than a pin-prick, the venom acts on nerves and body organs, producing severe muscle cramps, often in the abdominal region. The result is apt to be an emergency appendectomy.

Once while I was away, Ruth and Charlie decided to find out

just how aggressive a black widow might be. "We tried to make her bite a straw when we poked at her in the web," Ruth told me. "But all she did was pull in her legs and hang there. Then finally she dropped to the bottom of the jar. So we put her on the table, but she wouldn't bite the straw there, either. All she wanted to do was run away."

The story was quite different, though, a few days later. Lady produced a buffy-white bag of tough silk, about the size of a pencil eraser. Into it she placed several dozen pearly eggs. Shortly afterward, Ruth opened the bottle to take out the carcasses of the spider's past meals. This time, possibly because of eggs to guard, Lady darted at the tweezers with such force that Ruth jumped back. "Wow!" she muttered. "Talk about your split personalities!"

We decided that it must be such cases of impending motherhood that have caused the few dozen recorded deaths from bites by black widows. Just as I once saw a mother cottontail rabbit attack a fox as it snooped at her nest, so the retiring black widow must gain new courage when her potential brood is threatened.

One day in early June we stood looking at the beady little mother in her nondescript web. "It's hard to believe, isn't it?" mused Ruth.

"What's hard to believe?" Charlie asked.

"That the tangled web you see there is actually stronger and more elastic than steel. And that it was used for crosshairs in bombsights and gunsights. And that there are people in this world who actually raise black widows for a living. And that there's a little fly that sneaks in under momma's nose and lays eggs on the coccoon. And that parasitic maggots hatch from them and kill the little spiders. And that . . ."

She was still talking as I retired quietly from the room. Two days away was graduation, and I'd decided what my gift to her should be.

She could take Lady along with her when she left.

CHAPTER SEVEN

How Do You
Bathe a Loon?

THERE HAS BEEN an almost
endless stream through our bathtub. Not all of it has been water,
either. There have been creatures with feathers, fur, fins, scales,
wings, paddles—and even an occasional human being.

Years ago, when my pals and I used to catch frogs and turtles,
we learned how useful a bathtub could be. Its broad expanse gave
plenty of room for nearly any kind of critter and its slippery
sides prevented unscheduled escapes. If your catch was aquatic,
draw a few inches of water and there was an emergency pond
as well.

However, I hadn't figured that our bathtub would aid in our
national defense effort. It did, nevertheless, following a telephone
call to the Long Island Institute one February day.

"This is the Fairchild Engine and Airplane Corporation," a
voice said at the other end of the wire. "We found a bird
floundering around in an oily patch near the plant. Could somebody come and rescue it?"

I was puzzled. "Why, yes, we'd be glad to. But we have
classes here all day. Wouldn't it be possible for someone to put
it in a shoebox and bring it up to us?"

There was a silence. Then I heard a muffled conversation. Then
the voice returned. "Well, not exactly. You see, all the boys are
afraid of it."

HOW DO YOU BATHE A LOON?

"Afraid of it! How big a bird is it, anyway?"

"Looks to be about two and a half feet long. Gray and white. And about six inches of it is the sharpest bill you ever saw."

This sounded interesting. A bird like that was worth seeing, and I promised to be there during the noon hour.

I notified Connor Stephens, who was the Institute's bird specialist, and we headed for the Fairchild plant. A few minutes later, after suitable scrutiny at the gate followed by a high-level phone call to the main office, we were admitted. Then we were escorted to an asphalt ramp where a workman stood guard over a soggy mass of feathers.

"Okay, Bill. Thanks a lot," our guide told the workman. Then turning to us:

"Watch his beak. He'd put your eyes out if he got the chance."

It took just a glance to confirm what Connor and I had suspected. The bird was a common loon, apparently confused by a winter storm. Loons occasionally spent the winter in the waters off the Long Island shore. Spotting the oil-slicked asphalt, the loon had probably mistaken it for a puddle of water. Once down, it could not take off again because its feet were located so far to the rear that it needed a long stretch of water to get flying speed. And the more it floundered, the more it got covered with oil.

"Boy," said Connor, "that's the sorriest loon I've ever seen. His feathers are so matted that he couldn't fly if he was hitched to a balloon."

We threw an old blanket over the miserable creature, scooped him up, and I held him in my lap on the way back to school. Carefully I uncovered his head, mindful of the fish-spear he carried. His head, neck and back were dark gray. As much as I could see of his underparts were gray, too, though they should have been white. Gingerly I touched his feathers: they were cold and hard with grease.

We got back to school just as classes were beginning. So we put him in a box in a warm room during the afternoon session.

"What'll we do with him now?" I asked Connor after school was out for the day.

"Gosh, I don't know. My wife and I are supposed to go out for supper. Would you have time to take care of him?"

This was all I needed. "Sure. I'll see if we can get him cleaned up."

Half an hour later Peg met me in our living room as I entered the door with my large box. "What is it this time?"

"A loon. All covered with gunk. We've got to give him a bath."

"A *bath*? Where?"

"In the tub. Come on, Peg, be a sport. He needs our help."

Cautiously, she looked into the box. Her heart softened at once. "Oh, the poor thing. The poor, poor thing."

In we went to the bathroom. Soon our loon was drifting in six inches of tepid water.

"Now, how do you give a loon a bath?" Peg asked.

"Well, for a start, let's try some of your detergent. But you've got to watch out for that beak. He can do a good job on you with it."

So we poured a little Dreft in the tub. Like many wild creatures in their time of trouble, he seemed to understand what we were trying to do. Not once did he lance at us with that wicked beak, but submitted meekly to our attentions. Using a brush and washcloth, we laundered him thoroughly.

Finally, after three changes of water, he was fairly clean. "Now we'll let him go, yes?" asked Peg hopefully, surveying the black ring around her tub.

"No," clamored the children, who had been peeking over our backs during the process. "Let's keep him, Daddy. Can't we keep him?"

I wiped my hands on an old towel. "I'm afraid we've got to—for a couple of days at least. He's got to have time for the natural oil to get back in his feathers. Or he couldn't stay afloat. He'd drown in deep water."

HOW DO YOU BATHE A LOON?

Peg could see she was out-voted. "All right. Two days. But then—out he goes, whether he's changed his oil or not."

The next problem was food. Our books indicated that loons ate fish with an occasional frog or crustacean for variety. So we went to the market and bought a few of the smallest fish they had. But the loon surveyed the dead tidbits with as cold an eye as they turned up at him. Apparently we'd have to try live fish.

An all-night tackle store in Seaford catered to fishermen, and there we went and bought a handful of little killifish. Back home, I dumped them into the water with the loon.

They were an instant success. He cocked an eye, took brief aim, and picked them off in succession.

"Good," I said in satisfaction as we turned off the bathroom light and tucked the children into bed. "What more could you ask?"

"A bathtub," moaned Peg. "A nice, white, clean bathtub. For people."

Our loon stayed with us nearly a week. His feathers showed promise after two days, but they weren't glossy and slick the way I figured a water-bird's should be. Instead they were frizzly and curled, like the "before" pictures in the hair-tonic ads. Nevertheless the loon preened himself manfully, pressing his beak on the oil gland at his tail and threading the oil through every feather he could reach.

"See how guilty he looks," said Peg as we watched him one evening. "He knows we're waiting in line."

Finally it became apparent that we couldn't wait for the loon any longer. The children, of course, were happy not to have any baths, but Peg's viewpoint got dimmer by the day.

"Every time I look at that crazy loon in my tub I get itchy," she complained. "He's been here too long already. He's got to go."

So, reluctantly, I gave in. There was a local museum at Tackapausha Park in Seaford. Ed Morgan, its curator, was one of the finest naturalists on Long Island. We bundled the big bird up in a blanket and took him to Ed.

"How about a loon for your live-animal exhibit?"

"Fine. I'll just put him right in our big holding pool. We often keep water-birds—sometimes all winter. Got a couple of mergansers in there right now."

So we lowered the loon to the water. Gratefully he accepted his bigger quarters, swimming across the pool and coming out on the farther shore. Then, some fifty feet away from us, he proceeded to take a bath.

Like a sparrow at a puddle, he stood in the shallow water, showering it in a fine spray. Bobbing and shaking, he sprinkled the cold water all over himself.

This was almost too much for Peg. "Well, I like that!" she said. "Monopolized our tub for almost a week. And now, come to find out, the bathwater wasn't good enough for him!"

Our loon had the longest monopoly on our tub, but there were a number of short-term leases. A scaup duck was found wandering around on the Sunrise Highway, dazed and unable to fly. Apparently he'd been hit by a car. One of my students saw him and almost caused a traffic crackup when he stopped to rescue him. We put him in the laboratory sink, but I hesitated to leave him unattended overnight, so home he came for a night in the tub. By morning he'd recovered, splashed water all over the bathroom and created a general mess.

In summer we can quickly make a substitute for the bathtub, if it seems needed. All that's necessary is enough open ground to allow a few shovels of earth to be removed. Line the hole with pliofilm from a garment bag or other plastic material, fill it, and you've got an adequate pond. Sometimes even a birdbath can serve the same purpose.

Other denizens of our bathtub at various times have included a diamondback terrapin, a snapping turtle, a mess of catfish which were still living when I got them back from a fishing trip, a bullfrog and two smaller frogs (ending up as one very fat bullfrog the next morning) and, more recently, a frost-bitten muskrat.

HOW DO YOU BATHE A LOON?

Some students and I found the 'rat last winter, as we drove along a snowy gravel road near our Vermont farmhouse one bitter cold day. Somehow it had gotten in the road, and was unable to get back out because the sides were piled so high with snow. It had apparently been wandering for some time, for it was a long way from the nearest water. Naturally we got out to see if we could rescue it.

The 'rat, however, wanted none of our help. He crouched and sprang, leaping a foot off the ground, with those sharp teeth chattering. So I got an old dustrag from the car and played him like a bullfighter. At the same time one of the students slowly maneuvered around him with a heavy overcoat.

Finally the 'rat was in position. "Gotcha!" cried the boy as he tossed the coat on the muskrat. Following it with a flying tackle, he imprisoned the creature with such an embrace that I feared more for the muskrat than I did for the youngster.

We eased our prize into an old box and wrapped the box in the coat. Then we drove slowly, looking for a marsh or stream in which to release the muskrat. But every body of water was iced shut and covered with a foot of snow. There was nothing to do but take him home with me. After all, we couldn't let him go right out in the snow.

At home I filled the faithful bathtub half full of water, stood on a stool so I'd be free of any muskrat-leaps, and dumped the creature into the tub.

He took to the whole idea at once, swimming and diving from one end to the other. He stopped to scratch, swished around in the water, and finally settled down with apples and carrots we placed for him to eat. We admired the glossy coat with its thick underfur that dried almost instantly as he raised partially out of the water. Looking at him as he crouched and nibbled an apple, we saw the aptness of a description of him in one of my books: "The muskrat is a large, aquatic mouse, about 20 inches long, including a 7-inch vertically flattened tail."

Peg watched him for a while. "How are you going to keep him from getting out?"

"That's easy. Just have the water deep enough so he can't reach bottom with his feet without diving. Then he can't jump."

The muskrat showed no signs of trying to leave his tub. Just to be on the safe side, however, we closed the bathroom door for the night.

I was awakened in the morning a few minutes before the alarm was to go off. "Daddy," whispered Roger, "you'd better come and find the muskrat."

I glanced at Peg. Sound asleep. Or at least so she appeared. "All right, Roger. We'll get him."

But we didn't get him. We looked as long as we could before school. Remembering the way our woodchuck had hidden in plain sight, we looked in all the unlikely spots as well as the likely ones. We even lifted the sofa pillows and looked under them. Finally we had to leave for work—Peg to her kindergarten class and I to my Biology students at Vergennes high school.

"This is one of the times I'm glad to be away from home all day," said Peg as we closed the door. "I'd much rather face fifty five-year-old kids than that animated fur coat."

Our search that night was also futile. "Where is he?" asked Tom. "There's just no place left."

Of course there was one place. Just before preparing for bed that night, Peg had put a load of clothes in the washing machine. "Now what ails this washer?" she asked. "I turn it on, but nothing happens."

I checked the plug and fiddled with the dial light to make sure it was getting electricity. Then I pulled the machine away from the wall.

And there was our muskrat. Hunched in a corner of the metal housing around the mechanism, he blinked at my flashlight. He'd nibbled the insulation off the wires, and cut several wires clear through. The white ones, that is. The red, blue, green and black wires were completely untouched. How he did it without electrocuting himself is beyond my knowledge.

Tom tempted him out with a carrot, and we finally got him back in his tub. Then I spent an hour rewiring the machine. Finally, sometime around 1 A.M., the house quieted down.

Next day I made a muskrat cage. We put it outside in a sheltered spot, and managed to keep the web-footed little fellow for the rest of the winter. With spring, we let him go in a nearby swamp. And the activity around the bathtub has been remarkably dull lately. There's been nobody but human beings in it for almost two months.

But meanwhile we've used another dandy storage place: the refrigerator. Of course it helps if you have an understanding wife. It also preserves harmony in the family to have children who are trained to move the salamanders aside to get to the salad.

Salamanders and frogs often make their way to my icebox during the winter. Somebody finds one of the critters hibernating in his cellar, and soon it's brought to me. Usually I simply put it in my own cellar so it can go to sleep again until spring. Sometimes, though, I want to show it to my classes—so I pop it into the refrigerator for short-term keeping. This is not as bad as it seems, because the temperature just approximates that of many unheated cellars in winter.

As I say, my family is used to such situations, but many a visitor has been jolted to find a spotted salamander, or maybe two frogs, in a little dish just behind the butter.

I use my cold-storage creatures in various ways. Mostly I employ them to help my students become "collectors" in the sense that I am—making an animal yours by learning about its habits.

We inquire into the web of the foot of a frog, for instance. Painlessly wrapping him in a damp cloth to keep his skin moist, we stretch his foot out over a microscope stage. If he's too frisky, we give him a whiff of ether to calm him. Under the powerful lens we can see how wonderfully even a frog is put together. Arteries and veins and capillaries carry racing millions of blood cells in a bewildering maze of blood vessels.

Or we take a frog from the dark refrigerator into the sunshine and watch him change color. As his eyes respond to the bright light they tell the color cells in his skin to shrink in size. This causes him to change from darkest to lightest green—something which happens every dawn and yet is known but to few people.

Strange inhabitants are relatively common in our bathtubs and iceboxes by now. But the Reverend Jack Bursey surprised me completely with his wood turtle.

One late-winter day I happened to meet him in the postoffice in Bristol. "Spring must be just about here," he said. "My turtle's out of hibernation."

"Oh? Do you have a turtle?"

"Sure. Been with us seven years. Almost as big as a dinner plate. Out in the yard all summer, and sleeps in the bathroom closet all winter. Just poked her nose out today."

And the Burseys and the Roods aren't the only ones to have odd critters around the house. Not long ago I heard about a man who advertised in the paper for a house with an oversized bathtub. It seems that he needed a better place for his pet sea lion.

Recently, however, a little of the pressure has been taken off our domestic appliances. Up in the woods behind our house we've had a half-acre pond scooped out of the woodland, and, since the pond is fed by a fine little spring that's active all winter, there is always at least a little patch of open water. Now I know that Peg will insist that I take my flippered friends up there and let them go in all but the coldest weather.

So maybe the bathtub will be on a people-only schedule from now on.

CHAPTER EIGHT

Across the Bridge

WE CAN always tell when company's coming. There's a little plank bridge that goes across the river in front of the house. Every one of its planks grumbles and creaks under the weight of a car, so we need no doorbell to tell us we're about to have visitors.

Often it's possible to tell who's in the car, too, without looking. If it's a selectman or other town dignitary, the bridge fairly roars: they're here in high gear, and they mean business. If it's visitors from out of state, the bridge whispers slowly and thoughtfully as they savor to the fullest the lovely approach to my hundred acres. Janice's boyfriend's car rumbles impressively as he approaches for a date. Sometimes, hours later, the bridge creaks and squeaks accusingly if he's brought her home later than he should, no matter how carefully he drives over it.

We've been living in our little Vermont farmhouse across the bridge for eleven years now. It's a wonderful place for collectors like us, with our entire hundred acres a natural wildlife refuge of woods, meadows and river. Here we can "collect" with camera and binoculars as kingfishers dart up and down our river or deer graze at the edge of the south meadow.

In a way, I suppose, this could be called a third major period of my life. If my childhood and its wealth were a first period, and the four suburban years at the Long Island Institute were a second, it could be said that the wheel has finally come full circle.

Although Peg and I appreciated the many advantages of living in the suburbs, we both realized that there were drawbacks, too. Sometimes we got the feeling that we were amounting to little more than a couple of extra fares on the bus, another pushcart of groceries at the supermarket, or one more car in the bumper-to-bumper traffic on a Long Island highway. Finally, after I'd been teaching at the Institute for four years, we decided to try for the dream of many people—a home in the country. Now, at last, I can pursue my hobby while my children experience many of the same blessings I enjoyed in my youth.

During our years here, there has been almost as much traffic over our little bridge as there has been water below it. A sizable hunk of this traffic has been due to the curious or the information-seekers. Learning of such things as muskrats in our bathtub and blackflies in alcohol, they've come to see for themselves.

"I read your article in the latest issue of *Vermont Life.* Just stopped in to say 'hello.'"

"Thought you might like to take a close-up picture of this beetle grub, Ron. It fell out of a hollow log while Warner and I were sawing wood yesterday."

"Mother says you might like this hornet nest, Mr. Rood. It's empty—I think."

"Is this skunk sick or something? Billy and me found him down by the lumber mill yesterday and he ain't squirted even once."

One of the most startling critters to come across my bridge, however, arrived in a large glass jar. This was a five-inch, hairy South American tarantula. Patty Hier, who does most of my manuscript typing, picked it up—literally and figuratively—at work.

An acquaintance of hers, who works in a Burlington fruit store, had found it in a bunch of bananas. He managed to capture it in the jar, and took it across town to show to some of the girls in her office during the noon hour.

After they had dutifully screamed and shuddered, he announced he was going to destroy it. Patty, knowing I'd never forgive her if she let such a prize get away, stopped in the middle of a shudder.

"Oh, no—don't kill it! Give it to me!"

Thus it found its way to me. Out of sorts from its long trip from the tropics, it leaped on anything that was thrust into its jar. Those quarter-inch fangs, shaped like incurving tweezers, snipped pieces off broomstraws that I poked in through holes in the lid.

Our natural history encyclopedia informed us that tarantulas eat all kinds of prey. There is one, the bird-eating spider, that even captures small birds. Therefore a day or two later when one of the children brought home a dead mouse from beside the road, we put it in with the tarantula.

The mouse was an instant success. Pouncing so fast that we all jumped backward, the eight-legged monster bore its prize to the rear of the jar. In twenty-four hours the mouse was nothing but a few bones, some teeth and a mass of hair.

Now the huge spider was a different creature. Fat and satisfied, it merely moved out of the way when I poked at it. My book told me that tarantulas are essentially gentle, and seldom more poisonous than a wasp-sting. So, after making sure that its change of heart was not just a sham, I carefully tilted it out of the jar and onto my hand.

The outstretched legs covered my palm, my thumb and the lower joint of my fingers. The book indicated that such a large specimen was most likely a female. Then, as I held my breath, she slowly crawled off my hand to the tabletop and finally back into her jar.

This was my introduction to tarantula ways. Over the next year, however, I got to know her well. She remained gentle, and recognized my hand when I reached in to take her out of the jar. Like so many other things animate and inanimate in our lives, my tarantula had been terrifying only because I knew nothing about her.

Her gastronomic powers astounded me. I am sure that the first mouse we'd given her weighed nearly as much as she did. Not only was it a gigantic meal, but it stayed with her a long time. I got her in early June, fed her two days later, and couldn't persuade her to eat another thing until Christmas. This time she took a piece of hamburger the size of a large marble. A dead sparrow that someone had taken from his cat was given to me for her March meal. Then she didn't eat again until summer.

Like the black widow spider we'd had at the Institute, she often took a drink of water. I put a mayonnaise-jar cover in her big glass container and filled it with water. She drank from it by immersing the tips of those fangs and apparently sucking the liquid up through them.

For a while I had her at the Biology laboratory at Vergennes where I was teaching. The students were so fascinated with her that, far from having to protect them from the spider, I had to shelter the spider from the students. They took word back to their homes, and every few days I'd have to present my tarantula to another curious parent or brother or sister. And when spring vacation came, I was besieged with offers from students to take care of the tarantula while I went to Connecticut to visit my folks.

Back from my trip, I phoned the lucky student who'd been baby-sitting with my spider. "How did things go at the lab while I was gone?"

"Fine, Mr. Rood. But where'd you get the second tarantula?"

"The *second* one?"

"Sure. Same size as the first. There are two of them in the jar."

I tried to figure that one out. Perhaps someone had found another and put it in the same jar. Perhaps my fuzzy lady had laid a sac of eggs from which one had hatched and grown to adult size all in a week. Both suggestions sounded impossible.

At the lab the next morning I understood. There was no mystery at all. Nor was there a second tarantula. My eight-legged charge had merely followed an ancient custom, shared with the insects and the crustaceans. Growing slightly larger on her three-square-meals-a-year diet, she found her skin too small for her. So, splitting it along the back, she'd pulled herself out of it—legs, fangs and all. Now, in lifelike pose, her abandoned skin rested on a piece of wood in a corner of her jar. It was perfect, down to the eyes and the hair on the legs.

Possibly she injured herself in molting. Or perhaps some fumes from the laboratory assailed her delicate new skin. At any rate, although she ate one more meal in July, slightly more than a year since I obtained her, it took her twice as long to consume it. And a few days later when I reached in to touch her, there was no response. Carefully I removed her and put her in a container beside her empty skin. She's there today. Even though she's been dead a year, visitors still rumble over the river, wanting to see "that horrible tarantula I've heard about."

The variety of creatures across my bridge seems almost endless. Each one is interesting—often fascinating—and different from the last. In one week last summer we had two young chipmunks that had been rescued from a dog, a sticky wood turtle that had tried to cross a freshly tarred road, a blacksnake that a farmer had caught marauding a bird's nest, a wounded mourning dove, and a pair of half-grown hawks.

I usually release the animals as speedily as I can. This I do for two reasons. First, the Vermont Fish and Game department wisely frowns on the keeping of wild creatures protected by law. Second, the faster the animals are returned to their native habitat, the less they'll have to readjust to wild conditions.

When I can't release them right away, I often turn them over to the local game warden or take them out to nearby Dead Creek Wildlife Refuge for proper care. It's a serious mistake to keep a wild animal for even a short while. Even if you give it the right food and care, it quickly gets used to human beings. Then when you let it go, it's only half-wild and therefore can't protect itself.

Occasionally, instead of specimens coming to me, I have to go to them. This was the case one August morning when a little compact car drove across our bridge. Glancing out the window of my study, I saw a woman come toward the front door.

It was Eris Colomb, who had a summer cottage a few miles away. "Could you and your camera spare me half an hour?" she asked. "I have some wild ducks you might like to see."

The sun was bright and the day was good for photography, so I hopped in my car and followed her.

We got out at a little woodland cabin about three miles from town. In one corner of its tiny yard was a small wire enclosure. In the enclosure were nine ducklings.

"You'll never believe it when I tell you how they got here," she said, as I busied myself with the camera. "There are some beavers building a pond over on the other side of our property, and my husband and I have been interested in watching the pond grow as the beavers built their dam. A couple of months ago we were walking along the edge of the pond when we came across a nest of duck eggs. The water was rising up between the eggs. We knew the mother couldn't sit on them in the water and we figured that she couldn't take them to a new nest. So we felt justified in taking them ourselves."

Then she unfolded a most interesting tale. It began when they decided to hatch the ducks. Lacking an incubator, they seized upon the idea of an electric frying pan as a workable substitute. A book on duck-raising told them the proper temperature for the process was about 102°. So they set the control on the fry-pan handle and verified the setting with a thermometer.

At this point her son, who had joined us, took up the story. "The book told us we had to turn the eggs several times a day to keep the ducklings from sticking to the shell. So we put the eggs in the frying pan, put the cover on, and turned them when we were supposed to. And—what do you know? Every one of those eggs hatched three weeks later!"

I gasped in amazement at the incredible story. "Unbelievable!"

"—But true," Mrs. Colomb said. "There they are—nearly six weeks old."

"And," said her son proudly, "we didn't fry a single one."

I finished the pictures and went back home. "Now I've heard everything," Peg decided. "But still, if we can have loons in the bathtub, I guess other people can have ducks in a frying pan."

Several other times I've been called across my bridge to some other part of town. One June evening a woman arrived with two worried boys. "My husband's a logger," she explained, "and he wondered if you'd be interested in a pair of starving baby raccoons."

I looked in the back seat of the car. "Where are they?"

"Oh, they're not here. They're up where he was cutting some maple trees."

"How do you know they're starving?"

"Well, he and my son cut the tree yesterday morning. When it fell, they saw it was hollow. Up in the big hole was a nest, and it had two baby raccoons in it. They were blind and helpless. So they left them for their mother. But when they got back today, the mother hadn't come."

"How do you know she hadn't come?"

"They had crawled out of the nest and had gone about five feet through the leaves. And they were cold and crying."

I packed my camera and followed her to a farm several miles away. Sure enough, as we approached the spot, a thin little wail pierced the air.

"That's one of them now," said one of the boys. "If you ask me, they're starving to death."

The little raccoons fell quiet as they heard us scuffling through the leaves. Finally we found them—scrawny and naked, and completely at the mercy of any enemy that came along.

"Tell you what," I said, "let's put them back in their hole for

97

tonight. It'll be a warm evening anyway. Then, if you and your dad arrive tomorrow and they're still yelling like this, bring them to me. I'll think of some way to care for them."

We picked them up on an old slab of bark to keep the human scent off their bodies, and placed them in the tree. Then we stumbled our way out of the woods in the gathering dusk.

I hardly slept at all that night. Finally, as the darkness began to lessen outside, I got out of bed.

"Where in the world are you going?" Peg asked.

"Over to look at those raccoons. I've been worried about them ever since we left them there. It'd be a shame to have them starve to death. And even if the loggers did rescue them today, it'd be nightfall before the little fellows'd get anything to eat."

As I approached the tree my fears were realized. Now there were two wails, and they came from two different points. During the night the little raccoons had clambered out of the hole, dropped to the ground, and gone in search of the mother who didn't come. So feeble were they that they had gone scarcely three yards.

I picked them up. Their little black feet were cold to the touch. The slowness in their actions showed me they were chilled clear through. One of them had somehow injured its tail, perhaps the day before. There were a few blowfly eggs on the wound. No raccoon mother, I reasoned, would allow her baby to remain in such a condition without at least licking the wound.

That settled it. "All right, all right," I told them as I tucked them inside my shirt next to my skin where they'd be warm. "You can stop crying now. Everything's going to be just fine. Warm milk and a heat lamp will fix you up."

Then the three of us headed for home. A veery sang its flute-like song as I made my way back through the tangle of fallen trees. The sun was just rising over the hill by the time I got to the car.

Back at the house, Peg sweetened some milk with a little honey, warmed their bodies under the glow of a heat lamp, and soon had them nursing from a medicine dropper.

Now came the question as to what to do with them. A friend interested in conservation heard about them, and wanted them "just for a few days: then, when they don't have to be fed night and day, I'll turn them over to the authorities."

Wincing at this infringement of my own and official rules, I finally consented. "All right. They'd be an awful burden to a game warden when they're so young, anyway. But don't forget. Soon as they can feed themselves, out they go."

And so the story had a happy ending. But not always, of course, is this the case. And not always are "orphans" really abandoned. One time Cassius and Bea Guyett, with whom I often go hiking, were birdwatching with me along a mountain stream. We had our binoculars fixed on a flycatcher's nest in a river birch. I was just about to take a sideways step, still looking through the glasses, when Bea cried out.

"Don't move!" she said. "You'll step on the fawn!"

I followed her gaze to a spot of dappled brown right at my feet. There lay a newborn fawn, so still that we hadn't seen him in the fifteen minutes we'd been standing there.

Not a sign of life did he show. We couldn't even detect a motion of his little flanks to betray any breathing.

"Do you think he's dead?" Bea whispered.

"I don't know. I've never gotten so close to a baby deer before."

As if in answer to our question, a fly lit on the fawn's face. Crawling slowly, it made its way to that soft brown eye. The lid flickered ever so slightly. "He's alive!" said Bea. "He's alive, and right here at our feet."

Cassius turned slowly away. "I'm going back to the car to get my camera. Let's hope he doesn't get up and run."

We quietly left him undisturbed after we'd taken our pictures. "Do you suppose he's got a mother somewhere?" asked Bea anxiously.

We hoped this was the case. Later that day, when we returned down the trail, we decided we'd been right. His bed was empty and there were several large deer tracks in the mud that had not been there before.

"I guess it's just as the books all tell you," said Cassius. "It's best to leave young animals right where you find them. Everything's well in hand—if man doesn't upset the normal course of events."

This is especially the way with the young birds in summer. Probably as many trips across my bridge have been made for the supposed rescue of fledgling birds as for all other creatures combined. Two high-school students showed up one day with a young catbird as I was talking with a game warden who had stopped for a visit.

"How do we care for this bird? He must have fallen out of the nest."

My warden friend looked the little fellow over. Then he turned to the boys. "How far away from here was this bird found?"

"Oh, about three miles. Down at my house, in the back yard."

In a few minutes we had driven there in the warden's car. We released the catbird at the same spot where he'd been captured an hour before. And inside of three minutes, while we watched, his mother flew down from a cherry tree and thrust a caterpillar into his waiting beak.

"Well, I'll be darned," said one of the boys. "And I thought he was lost."

"You were right to be concerned," the warden told him kindly, "but he was just trying his new wings. Sort of like a boy in his dad's car away from home for the first time."

I was relieved that my friend's hunch had paid off so well. And I was gratified, too, that they'd thought of me when they'd been faced with a wild thing in apparent trouble.

I don't know who's going to come across the bridge next, but there's something I'm fairly sure of. It'll be somebody with a brand new critter for me to puzzle over.

Or at least it could be.

CHAPTER NINE

Breadline

THE FOLLOWING is a note copied from my journal:

"July 6, 1963. Several times in several days I have heard a muffled crash against the front window. Finally today I discovered the source—one of our young hairy woodpeckers who apparently thinks the window is a big hole in a tree.

"Right now he's clinging half dazed to the side of one of our sugar maples where he flew after hitting the window and picking himself up off the ground. (Took three close-ups with the camera.)"

Nothing outstanding, at first thought, about that news note. Lots of people have had birds fly into windows. Often, during the breeding season, a male bird will fight his reflection in a window until he's exhausted. But this was a youngster still in spic-and-span juvenile plumage, and not supposed to be interested in such things as other male birds. And he was, moreover, what Peg and I called with some pride *our* woodpecker. We'd watched his progress almost from the day he was hatched.

Actually, we may be able to point out to a visitor more than a dozen occupied birdnests right around the house any time in the breeding season. This is not due to any magic formula at all, but simply because once we got lazy.

It seems that previously we had always hauled in our bird-feeding trays when the leaves had emerged and the grass was green. But this particular year I lacked the energy to take the trays in, so they stood deserted in the yard.

One day Peg glanced out as a lone nuthatch was reminiscing over an empty tray. "Why don't you either take that thing down or put some food in it?" she asked. "That nuthatch came back to see if any food was left. See how disappointed he is. I bet if you put some food out, he'd take it just as he does in winter."

So I put a little suet in the holder and sprinkled a few sunflower seeds on the tray. I felt a little silly, because the act of feeding the birds is a winter ritual. I associated it more with skis and snow shovels then I did with lilacs and lawnmowers. But, as I said, I was feeling lazy. It was easier just to dump some food on the tray than to take the tray down and store it in a safe place.

This was several years ago. We've been feeding the birds year round ever since.

It used to be that we smiled at the gaudy pictures on the birdseed bags in the stores. There you'd see portraits of all kinds of birds, with the implication that a bird-feeding program would soon have your snowscape alive with color and song. All you had to do, apparently, was put out a shot of Big Boy Bird Breakfast. Then all the tanagers, orioles, warblers and bluebirds would magically return from the south at twenty below zero and gladden your bird-feeding heart until the first shivering song sparrow returned two months later.

We smiled once, that is. Now we do not. We'd still be surprised if we saw an oriole in Lincoln much before May, but we *do* have them at our feeders from then on. And scarlet tanagers. And robins and catbirds, too. In fact, by keeping our feeding station going all year, we've managed to attract a surprising number of summer birds and hang on to our winter ones as well.

Birdfeeders, by the way, are not just for country-dwellers. Birds are wonderfully mobile, and will find their way to a shelf outside an apartment window. Even a cardboard box will do.

As for food, canary or parakeet seed may be used if regular feed is not available. Breadcrumbs do not seem too successful, though: graham-cracker crumbs or other whole-cereal materials apparently are more acceptable. So are doughnut crumbs. Or hang a stale doughnut from a convenient place by a string. It swings in the breeze in such a way that the English sparrows seldom bother it, but other small birds will pick at it for days. The fat in the dough, combined with its sweetness, appears to be relished by many birds.

I often vary the standard diet of seeds and suet. Peanut butter mixed with uncooked rolled oats makes a fine food that can be pressed into cracks in the bark of trees—or bricks of a house, if you live in the city. The birds will work at this mixture for hours, trying to extract the last morsel. However, peanut butter must not be used alone, for it tends to cake in the tiny stomachs, causing the birds to become crop-bound.

There have been a number of means devised to control unwanted guests at birdfeeders. Sometimes squirrels became a nuisance. They can be discouraged to some extent by putting a large metal flange or guard beneath the feeder if it's on a post. There are also feeders having a hinged-door arrangement. When a heavy creature such as a squirrel or jay lands on the platform, the door swings shut. The weight of lighter birds does not affect it.

Our year-round feeder activity hinges on the fact that birds and animals are not above taking the easy way. If, in their search for insects or weed seeds, they come across a piece of suet tacked to a tree, or a chunk of food placed on a shelf outside a window, they'll probably take a bite or two. Then if the food's there the next time around, they'll take another bite. And if this is supplemented with fruit and seeds put out for them, they may decide to settle down near by and raise a family.

Of course the laws of elbow-room still hold. Two pairs of downy woodpeckers won't nest in our old dying maple just because there's some suet handy. They'd squabble so much that one pair would soon move away. But where the decrepit tree might have enough insects to support one family of woodpeckers, a side dish of suet and sunflower seeds might attract a pair of chickadees, too. Birds of the same species need what the biologists call "breeding territory" of a certain size, but birds of different species may nest within a few feet of each other in peace. Thus, by means of our suet subsidy, we bring them together.

There's an old maple, for instance, that leans 'way out over the river in front of the house. Last summer there were five nests in operation there: a flicker in the old stub at the top, a downy woodpecker in a neat little hole halfway down, a robin in the crotch, an oriole's swaying bower on a limb far out over the water, and a chipmunk hole at the roots. Their owners all paid visits to the feeding station—even the chipmunk, which hid so many sunflower seeds underground that the whole lawn would rise if they sprouted at once.

My children and I were sitting on the lawn one day, watching the efforts of a catbird as she strove to keep ahead of her four flourishing young ones. "Three and a half minutes that time, Dad," said Alison as we timed the interval between visits to the nest. "Boy, those birds must really work to find enough bugs for the babies."

Then, as we watched, the catbird dropped down to the suet. She took a few quick bites, wiped her bill on a piece of bark and went back to her food-hunting.

"Coffee break," laughed Alison.

Roger was puzzled. "But why doesn't that catbird save time and trouble and just give a piece of suet to each of her babies? Then she wouldn't have to look so hard for insects."

We finally decided—and our books later confirmed—that fiercely growing little bodies need the proteins and minerals represented by insects and spiders, rather than the more restricted diet of pure suet-fat. A young bird may increase its weight tenfold in as many days. So our summer feeder didn't lessen the war on insects. You could almost say it kept it going at top speed.

Favorite among our birds are the chickadees. Almost completely without fear, they fly readily to my hand when I hold out some food for them. On balmy days in winter I have my study window open, with a few sunflower seeds on the tabletop inside. The chickadees come right into the room, pick out a seed, and fly to a nearby tree. There they hold it in their black little feet, picking at it until they've split the husk, and extract the meat.

One day I was running low on their usual food and decided to try a new diet. We like to nibble on the kernels of pumpkin seeds, and dry a quantity of them every fall. Now I placed a few on the tabletop and waited for developments.

One of the black-and-white birds flew down. He looked in vain for sunflower seeds, but the last one had been taken. So he picked up a pumpkin seed. Flying to a branch, he began to hammer away at it.

These seeds, however, didn't seem to split as readily under the impact of the little black bill. He whacked away for a while and then shifted its position. More whacks, and he looked at it in disgust. Flying to the main trunk of the tree, he hid the offending seed in the bark.

Now began a shuttle between tree and table. One by one he picked up the pumpkin seeds and tucked them away in the tree. Finally, when the last one was gone, he glared at me.

"Now," his manner plainly said, "bring on your sunflower seeds. Let's get back to business."

We've had as many as twenty chickadees around our feeder at once. One will perch at the edge of the tray and open his beak at any others that dare come near. Since chickadees often travel in family groups, this may be the patriarch of them all, telling Junior and Momma and Aunt Susie to wait their turn.

Then, when he flies away, the next in line may try the same stunt. But maybe his attitude lacks the air of authority, and so there's often a squabble as to who gets the next seed.

Birds come in waves to our feeding station—not only according to the time of year, of course, but also according to the time of day. One February morning Peg looked out into the gray dawn and called me to the window.

"What kind of birds are those out there on the ground?"

I could just barely make out their dark shapes against the snow. "I don't know, Peg. We'll have to wait until it gets a bit lighter."

Finally we were able to identify them. They were tree sparrows, those little red-capped birds with the black stickpin adorning a whitish breast.

The tree sparrows remained there nearly half an hour before any other birds showed up. Then came the chickadees, followed finally by the blue jays and English sparrows.

This gave Peg an idea. "You've been wondering how you'd get the tree sparrows fed without English sparrows moving in on them and swiping it all," she said. "Why not put some seeds out the night before? Then the tree sparrows would have their food the first thing in the morning."

We've done this ever since. The little tree sparrows are the early birds that get the seeds. Then when the pesky, blatant English sparrows arrive with their bankers' hours, they have to take what's left.

The most handsome visitor to our feeding station is the blue jay. Tough, strong and husky, he can whack a new piece of suet to shreds in a few hours. And he cuts the corners with the sunflower seeds, gulping down a whole dozen while a chickadee is opening one. Naturally he's not always received with enthusiasm, especially when he arrives with ten or a dozen of his classmates.

We've had a running battle with the jays in an effort to keep them from monopolizing the whole feeding operation. "Drill an inch-and-a-half hole in an empty coconut shell," my father had advised years ago, "and hang it up. Then, when you fill it with sunflower seeds, the chickadees and nuthatches will be able to get

106

them. The jays won't be able to cling to the smooth shell as they swing back and forth."

Remembering his suggestion, I drilled, filled and hung. Sure enough, the smaller birds perched on the edge of the hole, reached in for a seed, and flew away with it. The jays tried the same thing, but their bulky bodies were too clumsy. However, this didn't hold them back for long. They soon learned to half-cling, half-hover in the air, beating their wings to maintain their position while they gobbled the seeds.

Tom looked at the less-than-perfect results. "How about putting a metal roof up so their wings hit it on the upbeat, Dad? They wouldn't be able to flutter in the air if you did that."

So I took one of the sheet-metal racks that Peg uses in cooking pots to keep things from burning down. I hung it in such a way that it projected down over the hole like the visor of an oversized cap. "Ha!" I cried at the jays through the windowpane as they surveyed it in surprise. "Think your way out of *this* one!"

They thought. It didn't take long, either. One jay, blundering in his attempts to hang on, spilled a few seeds out the hole. Dropping to the ground, he quickly picked them up. Then he flew up and spilled a few more.

The others soon caught on. By midafternoon the coconut shell was bouncing like a punching bag as the jays careened into it and picked their prizes off the ground.

My latest gambit in the contest is making a cage for the shell. Using some rectangular woven chicken wire with one-by-two-inch mesh, I made a big wire cage of the stuff and enlarged the mesh with my fingers just enough to admit the small birds but not the larger bodies of the jays.

It has worked very well so far. It's been up two weeks and no jay has solved the puzzle yet. And I'd be willing to place a bet that they don't, either. A small bet, that is. And no odds. Jays are too smart.

One time on a trip to Crater Lake National Park, a fellow

camper gave us further evidence of jay mentality. The Clark's nutcracker, looking like a small black-and-white crow, is a constant visitor to the Park's picnic areas. It's so bold that it may perch right on the table, sometimes even taking a sandwich or a doughnut. A small cousin of the nutcracker is the gray, or Canada, jay. Known by lumbermen as "camp robber" or "whiskey jack," it, too, perches on the table in hopes of filching a piece of bread. When the larger nutcracker arrives, though, the jay keeps a respectful distance.

According to Park Department rules, you are not supposed to feed any birds or animals, as it makes them dependent on man for handouts. "However," our camper friend said, "we were feeding a bag of peanuts to a little ground squirrel and a gray jay so my son could take some pictures. A Clark's nutcracker hopped up and demanded his share. We of course obliged, while the jay and squirrel retreated.

"The nutcracker was probably already filled to bursting from the other tables around us. He took the peanuts and just flew to a nearby pine with them. Then he stuffed them in a knothole. But that jay was watching him. So as fast as the nutcracker put a peanut in and flew away, the jay took it out. I bet the nutcracker would have packed ten pounds of peanuts in that tiny knothole if our bag hadn't gone empty—and if the jay hadn't got full."

Unfortunately there's a rascal's heart beneath the jay's jaunty exterior. One time I saw a yellow warbler flying in and out of the bushes in desperation. Running to the scene, I discovered a blue jay calmly picking the baby warblers out of the nest and dropping them to the ground. Another time I surprised a jay in the act of pecking holes in the eggs of a song sparrow. So I view our winter jays with mixed feelings.

Yet I know they have a very definite and necessary place in the scheme of life on my hundred acres. One spring afternoon I suddenly heard the blue jays burst into a chorus of excited screams. As I rushed to the window, a gray form hurtled by: a Cooper's hawk, hunting low, zoomed into the air, banked away, and disappeared.

Not a bird moved for several minutes. Then, slowly, the life around my feeder returned to normal. Of course the hawk, too, has his place in the necessary chain of life. Without him, the smaller birds would have little to hold them back and would undergo a disastrous population explosion. That's why I put out suet and seeds where the jays can get them, even while I cover the coconut shell.

I know this may mean tragedy for some yellow warbler or song sparrow some day, but that's in the normal scheme of the life they lead. After all, jays and songbirds got along for eons together before we began to intervene. Therefore I feed the jays. Not because I love them, but because I love the bluebirds and warblers whose lives they help control in a way far beyond man's wisdom.

The highlight of our bird-feeding year occurs when the parents bring their young out into the world. Then we see just how hard they've been working at raising a family. The adults' plumage is faded and worn, while that of their offspring is bright and clean. Often the young seem larger than their parents, and it makes us laugh to see a slim mother followed by three or four fat youngsters wherever she goes.

They usually bring their babies to the feeding station in a day or two. "Now, children," you can almost hear them saying, "this is suet. And these are sunflower seeds. They're both good to eat. Watch me, and you'll learn how it's done."

But the babies are slow to learn. Or maybe they just don't want to. The female hairy woodpecker whose son came to grief against our window would arrive at the feeder day after day. She'd be followed by her two noisy boys, who would sit within a foot of her on the tree trunk while she picked pieces off the suet. Clamoring at the top of their lungs, they'd yell for it until she presented

109

them with a chunk. Down it would go—and they'd shout for more.

"Lazy lummoxes," said fifteen-year-old Tom as he watched their mother's efforts. "Why don't they learn to take care of themselves?"

"Don't worry," said eighteen-year-old Janice, home for a day from her summer job. "They will."

And apparently they have, for as I type this in early March I can hear a male hairy woodpecker drumming loudly on a dead limb outside. Perhaps it's my blundering adolescent of last year, now grown to maturity and announcing his intention of starting a family of his own in the tree above my year-round breadline.

CHAPTER TEN

Mechanical Mice

"Dad, when a mouse is out alone in the woods and a fox is hunting him, is the mouse afraid?"

"I don't know, Alison. I guess to answer that, you'd have to be a mouse yourself."

"I hope they're not afraid. It must be awfully scary running around in the leaves at night."

We finally decided that only those creatures which could think into the future would be afraid. And since the mouse probably didn't pause to consider all the things that might happen, its short life was probably quite uncluttered by fear.

This had been pretty well proved to me in my grandfather's barn years ago. My brother and sister and I used to climb up through an opening into the hayloft and lie there looking down at the cows. Often we'd see mice come out of the walls and rummage around below us, looking for grain. One day Irma and I were watching one of the little rodents as it approached a dark spot near an upright beam. As it got closer, we saw to our horror that the dark spot was Felix, my grandfather's cat.

We both shouted a warning. At the same instant the cat sprang. But our warning had been just quick enough to make

111

the mouse jump, so the cat missed his aim. His claws caught the mouse for an instant—then the little creature wriggled free and disappeared.

We were enraged. "Scat!" we yelled at the surprised cat, whose chief job was most likely the control of these very mice. Poor Felix took for the barn door as if a can were tied to his tail.

"How bad do you suppose he hurt the mouse?" Irma asked.

"I don't know. But I bet he scared him plenty."

From habit, we'd been conversing in low tones. Now we fell silent and turned our gaze to the barn floor again. No sooner had we settled down than a mouse scurried across the floor. He was followed by another. They frolicked for a moment, then began to poke in the chaff for more grain.

To our surprise we saw that one of the mice was the little one which had just escaped. We could see two white scratch-marks along his flank where the claws had raked the fur.

"Golly," said Irma. "He didn't stay scared long, did he?"

I was to remember her words years later when a Cooper's hawk rocketed past the birdfeeder in the front yard of my house in Vermont. Although the little songbirds froze in their tracks, they were moving unconcernedly about in a few moments, with the hawk apparently forgotten.

We've noted this marvelous ability to forget everything but the present in creatures we've brought into the house, too. A chipmunk our son Tom found was nibbling peanut butter and rolled oats within ten minutes of the time we put him into a little wire cage. A chickadee which once flew in the open window of my study somehow forgot the way out, and trapped himself against the upper glass. There he fluttered wildly until a fly, disturbed by his efforts, buzzed past. Instantly the chickadee took a bead on the fly, snapped him up—and then continued his struggles.

"Opportunist!" chuckled Janice as we watched this strange quirk in a bird supposedly scared to death. And this could well be the guiding principle of many of my wild neighbors: seize today, and let tomorrow care for itself.

Two years ago I took a refresher course in Biology at Dartmouth which included a section on animal behavior. It was suggested that we observe the creatures around us, trying to see if we could predict how they'd act in certain circumstances. I took notes on the actions of many of the wild creatures, and read all I could find about many more. As in so many things of our world, the facts staggered the imagination as much as any fiction.

I had been curious about wasps and bees, for instance, ever since childhood. Once I had made the mistake of hitting a wasp nest with my head when I was playing hide-and-seek. As I recall, I gave myself away a few minutes earlier than I'd planned. And I'd seen wasps and hornets dive-bombing our cow as she wandered in the meadow. It had always intrigued me as to why she wasn't panicked by their attentions.

Finally I figured out the answer. The wasps were catching the flies on Clover's back and chewing them to bits.

It remained for my Animal Behavior course, however, to show me what the wasp was really doing with the insects she caught. The adult extracts the body juices from the fly for its own use, and then takes the solids back to the nest for the young. When she presents food to the grubs, they produce a little bubble of saliva. The wasp seems to wait for this bubble and laps it up readily. Then she presents the little patty of fly-burger to the next grub, receives a bubble of saliva, and so on.

I learned, too, that the drone, or male, wasp does not forage for food, but relies on that brought in by the females. Nor is he above robbing the cookie-jar himself when he gets the chance. Walking up to a grub in its little paper cell, he tickles it as if he were about to present it with some food. The little grub obligingly produces a bubble of saliva. The drone laps it up quickly and goes on to the next victim.

Apparently this mutual-feeding operation seems to be a strong

113

force in holding the many inhabitants of a nest together. Biologically it is known as trophallaxis. Many scientists who have studied the subject feel that a hornet protecting the nest is in much the same situation as a dog protecting a bone: those little living lollipops in their paper cells must be preserved at any cost.

Trophallaxis, I learned, could sometimes backfire. Intrigued by what I'd found about the social insects, I decided to study their movements further. So I dug up an anthill and carefully singled out the queen with about two hundred of her "subjects." Then I put them in an all-glass case with soil from the anthill and let them remake their home. Little tubes at the top allowed me to introduce food and water. When they were well established in their new home, I invited Peg to watch the ants in action.

Dutifully she peered at them through the magnifying glass. "I thought you said you had just ants," she said.

"That's right. Two hundred of them."

"Well, what's this bug doing in the anthill, then?"

"Probably got in when I put some soil in from the nest. They'll capture the bug soon as they discover it."

"Maybe. But they must have discovered it already. It's running around right in the middle of the ants and they pay no attention."

Curious, I took the magnifier. Soon I saw the insect. It appeared to be a slender beetle about the size of an ant. As I watched, one of the ants stroked it with its antennae and then licked the beetle's body. Then both insects went their separate ways.

I reported the strange occurrence to my professor. "Ant guests," he said. "Otherwise known as inquilines. Your little guest has taken advantage of the ants' fondness for good-tasting body secretions. It probably has an attractive flavor. Ants take their guests with them if the colony is forced to move to a new location. Even the hordes of army ants have inquilines with them as they march."

But it seems that the inquiline is often there on shady business, for, once inside the nest, it feeds on the eggs and young of the ants. So it's like a little Trojan horse, or an enemy within the

114

gates. Get enough inquilines and they'll finish a nest of ants. Usually, however, the queen ant lays so many eggs that a few of these guests don't matter.

Through the years in my work with wild creatures, I've found many more examples of activity which may seem strange to us but which make the animal world ever new and fascinating. One summer we visited the Wichita Mountains National Wildlife Refuge in Oklahoma. We'd found the campsite we liked; Peg and Janice had brushed it smooth with a little broom, and Roger and Alison were busy putting out tent stakes. Tom and I pulled the folded tent out of the car.

Suddenly Roger and Alison squatted down. We could see that they were looking intently at something on the ground. "Whatcha got, kids?" I asked.

"Don't know, Dad. Looks like two bugs pushing a brown marble."

We brought the tent nearer and laid it down. " 'Two bugs and a marble?' " I asked. "What do you mean?"

"These," said Alison, pointing to an active duo of insects on the sun-baked earth. "They're having a tug of war or something."

I bent down for a better look. They were the industrious beetles known as tumblebugs, or dung beetles. They'd shaped and pushed a bit of buffalo dung until it was a little half-inch sphere. Now they rolled it along—one beetle pushing from behind, the other pulling it from the front.

Our neighbor at the next campsite saw us absorbed in the strange little scene. He strolled over to see what interested us. "Tom-Bill bugs," he grinned. "You see them around here a lot."

" 'Tom-Bill bugs?' You mean tumblebugs?"

"No. Tom-Bill bugs. You watch. They help each other out. Tom pulls. And Bill pushes."

Roger was puzzled. "But why do they push it around, anyway? Are they playing or something?"

"Nope. They get that ball of dung to the right spot and bury

115

it. They lay their eggs on it so their grubs will have something to eat."

Just then a little gust of wind swept by, whirling up twigs and dust. It tumbled the tumblebugs, too, spilling them in separate directions. Bill—or was it Tom?—found the dung first and quickly began rolling it along as fast as his six legs would work. Tom—or was it Bill?—searched back and forth, but not a sign of the ball did he find. Bill had hijacked it. Whether by accident or design, he was off in a new direction, leaving his erstwhile partner quite literally in the dust.

We watched the two of them for a while and then turned to the business at hand. The last time we looked, Tom was still searching while Bill scuttled down the path with his stolen prize.

And what causes these odd quirks of behavior, which make insects and other creatures so interesting? Instinct. Activity that's present in wild creatures without their having to practice it. They do it right the first time—like the caterpillar spinning its cocoon or the spider making her web. Bit by bit, action by action, they follow a set, inborn pattern until the job's completed.

Sometimes even instinct goes wrong. If the pattern is interrupted, the insect may have to go back and start over, like a little girl I once saw in a piano recital. Halfway through her solo she forgot what came next. She sat and looked at the keys for a moment, but they seemed to tell her nothing. "Heck!" she exclaimed—and began all over again.

There are insects that behave the same way. One of the outstanding examples is a certain digger wasp. This little creature digs a hole in the ground. Then it searches until it finds a grasshopper. It stings the grasshopper to paralyze it, then brings it back to the hole. Here it will lay eggs on it so they'll have fresh 'hopper to eat when they hatch out.

Arriving at the nest, the wasp leaves the grasshopper at the edge of the hole. Then it goes below for a last inspection before it takes its victim down. If you wait until the wasp has gone below and then move the 'hopper a few inches away, you upset things completely. The wasp pulls the grasshopper back to where it was—and goes below for her inspection a second time. Move the 'hopper away again and the wasp goes through the same routine. Apparently she can't go on to the next step until the preceding one is over and done with.

Instinct may insist on pushing straight ahead even if it would be wiser to meet changing conditions. This was the case with one of the first mud-dauber wasps I ever saw, when my little brother and I noted it on the wall of our barn back in Connecticut. This wasp builds hollow cells about an inch long and a quarter-inch in diameter. Made of mud, the cells are stuffed with spiders which the wasp has stung and paralyzed as food for her off-spring. Several of the cells may be stacked together on a wall or under a ledge. When the female has filled each cell, she puts a little patty of mud in the end as a stopper.

We watched as the metallic-blue insect finished her last cell. As she flew away, we bent to inspect her work. The cell was crammed full of paralyzed spiders.

"Probably she'll seal it with mud when she returns," I told Jimmy.

"She'll have to. She could never get another spider in there," he replied, poking carefully at the entrance to the cell. Then he grinned. "Just think of how disappointed she'd be if she came back and couldn't find the nest."

This gave us an idea. Carefully, with a watchful eye for the wasp's return, we scraped the nest from the side of the building. Then we sat back to see what the female would do.

Shortly she returned. Flying straight to the site of the nest, she landed with a little blob of mud clasped under her chin.

She paused scarcely an instant. Then she unloaded her burden in the spot where the cell should have been. Patting it out into a little disk, she shaped it and prodded it. Even if the cell was no longer there, she put the lid where it was supposed to go. Then,

117

circling around her work a few times as if to give it a final inspection, she flew away.

We sat quietly a few minutes more, but she didn't return. Finally we got tired of waiting.

"Gosh, Ronny," my brother said as we left, "do you suppose that's all she's going to do? I thought she'd start all over again."

But she didn't return. When we went back the next day nothing had changed. The blank wall still remained with its pathetic little single patty of mud. The insect mother had done her duty. The inbuilt tape-recorder that instructed her had run its course. There was no rewinding.

Years later, in that course on animal behavior, I mentioned the strange occurrence to my professor. "Animal instinct is often like that," he said. "It does a wonderful job if everything goes all right. And normally, of course, everything would. But face an insect with an unusual condition and it may be powerless to cope with it."

There was something strangely human about that situation as I discussed it with my instructor. Later I recalled what it was. A friend of mine the year before had taken a training course to become an insurance salesman. He learned a careful sales pitch designed to lead the prospect from "not interested" to "where do I sign?" in one smooth operation. The talk began with this question: "Mr. Prospect, do you realize that every day you live, your responsibilities are *decreasing*?" This was supposed to intrigue the prospect so much that he wanted to hear more. Whereupon, of course, you had him.

On his first day out in a supposedly hostile world, my friend had the good fortune to call on an executive who was in the market for insurance. "What I want to know, young man," snapped this worthy gentleman, "is this. How much do you fellows want for a ten-thousand-dollar endowment policy on a fourteen-year-old girl?"

The salesman was caught completely off base. But only for a moment. Then the careful training of the past weeks flooded back on him. "Mr. Stevens," he began, "do you realize that every day you live, your responsibilities are decreasing? . . ."

My friend's reaction hardly fitted the situation at all. It made just about as much sense as that little mud-dauber wasp and her finishing touch.

On the other hand, I've seen a number of cases where the individuals concerned have shown a surprising adaptability. One morning I was walking along the sidewalk in the city of Burlington. I noticed a cat crouched beneath a parked car, apparently asleep. "That's a risky place to take a nap," I remarked to the policeman on the corner.

"You'd think so," he said, "if you didn't know just how that cat gets its living. It just creeps along under the parked cars until it comes to a place where some sparrows or starlings are feeding in that stuff by the curb.

"One of my friends even saw it catch a pigeon this way. I'm sure nobody in town owns that cat, but it's just as fat as my cat at home."

Another animal that had learned to profit on the parking lot was a gray squirrel we once saw at a state forest park. As we pulled into an empty spot not far from the wooded edge of the lot, the squirrel came bounding up to the car. It jumped up on the front bumper. We could hear its sharp claws scratching the metal for a moment; then it dropped off and went to the next car.

Carefully we opened the doors. Slowly getting out where we could watch the little animal, we learned the reason for its strange behavior: it was visiting the front of every car on the parking line, picking the insects off the bumpers and radiator grilles.

There is also the case of the stowaway toad. I had found the toad out on the lawn at dusk, and put him in a large pail with some grass in the kitchen. I planned to take some close-up pictures of him in the morning. But I completely forgot him.

The next evening Peg brought me the pail. "Found this tipped over on the floor. It's got some grass in it, but that's all. Would

119

you mind telling me what else was in it so I'll know if I dare go into the kitchen again?"

"Just a toad, Peg. Jack must have been sniffing it and tipped the thing over."

We enlisted the help of the children, and the search was on. Jack was a big help, too, assisting in his best canine fashion, poking his wet nose into our faces whenever we got down to look under the furniture. Yet no toad was to be found.

I called off the search, assuring the youngsters that toads and frogs can go for days with no food at all. Then I settled down in the living room to read.

Soon I became aware of an unusual number of insects buzzing around the table lamp. The children were in the other room. "Did any of you kids leave a window or door open?" I asked.

"No windows, Daddy. Just doors. We're letting the toad find his way outside again."

Finally I persuaded them to forget the toad and close the doors, and turned to my book again.

Before long I began to hear a faint noise at my feet. It sounded like water dropping on a sheet of cardboard. "Blip!" it went, and "blip!" again.

Finally it penetrated my consciousness to the point where I looked down to see what was causing it. There sat our missing amphibian on the rug. His warty sides bulged as he took aim at a moth that had bumped into the lamp and fallen to the floor.

"Blip!" went his sticky flap of a tongue as it shot out and swatted the moth. Attached at the front of his mouth, its free end could reach an inch beyond his body. He'd flip the moth back into his throat, swallow mightily, and pull those huge eyes down into the roof of his mouth to help the insect on its downward way.

"Thanks a lot for bringing me in here," his manner plainly said. "Never had such a good meal in my life."

Bufo, as we called him after his scientific name, stayed with us for more than a week. By day he hid beneath the piano. As soon

120

as it was dark enough I turned on the desk lamp for him.

One day, though, Janice came home from her summer job and sat down to play the piano. Bufo endured it all right, but apparently liked his music in smaller doses. The next day he was tucked into a dark corner of the living room.

After that he wouldn't stay in any one place, so we let him go. Obviously he distrusted the underside of every piece of furniture in the house. I guess he never knew when it might burst forth in the latest beat.

It's interesting to inquire into the subject of animal behavior on your own. Note carefully the web of a spider, for instance. Then pull part of it from its moorings and see if the repairs resemble the original.

Or discover the relative importance of scent in the daily rounds of ants by drawing your finger firmly across one of their pathways. Some types will become confused at this interruption of their scent trail—even though the path continues after only half an inch— while others possibly see the familiar road ahead and travel on with scarcely a pause.

Or put a vertical sheet of clear glass in the middle of an aquarium so it divides the space in half. Then, after the fish have become accustomed to the glass, take it out of the water. They won't cross the boundary, even if it's no longer there. (This last, by the way, is a good conversation-piece if you have a home aquarium. Your guests won't be able to figure it out.)

We can give all kinds of explanations, I suppose, for squirrels that visit the front of cars, garden toads that live under a piano until some music-lover drives them out, insects that lick each other like postage stamps, and mice that play in the very teeth of danger. My Animal Behavior professor would use such words as "instinct," "trophallaxis," "adaptation," and "acquired behavior."

There was a time when I'd have recoiled from a view that made the fascinating creatures around us seem like nothing but a bundle of reflexes. However, Peg has put it in the right perspective.

"I read somewhere that a sunset was due merely to the effect of light rays on droplets of water and pieces of soot and dust in the atmosphere," she said as we gazed west toward the Adirondacks one evening. "So the dirtier the air, the prettier the sunset. But somehow, even though it's all explained, I still manage to enjoy it."

American toad gathers a tidbit with his trick tongue (National Audubon Society).

Necessary to the balance of nature are the blue jay, *top left* (American Museum of Natural History), and the sparrow hawk. The white-footed mouse climbs trees and jumps like a squirrel (American Museum of Natural History); *below,* with two students, about to release a turtle that had become a class pet.

The "pony swim" across the narrows to Chincoteague (photographed by James Watson). Peg gathering famed oysters for an appetizer, and, *right*, Roger with Little Fellow back home in Vermont.

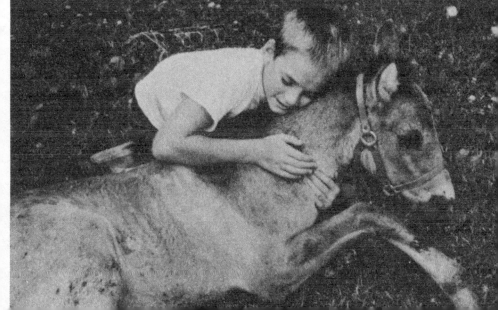

Trust between man and animal—Pokey on my shoulder (by John Smith). Visiting ermine, *opposite,* photographed through my study windowpane.

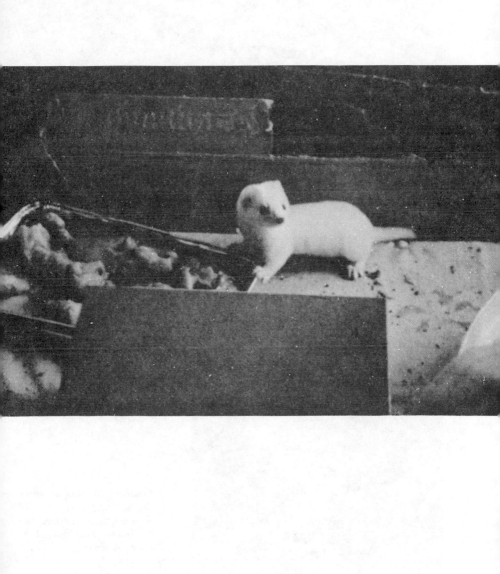

Feeding an orphan wood-
chuck and, *right*, full-
grown spring peepers (both
American Museum of Na-
tural History).

CHAPTER ELEVEN

"Man Is a Mamma"

MY FAMILY often helps me correct Biology tests. This is not as detrimental to the educational process as it sounds. If the test is multiple-choice, true-false, or similar in form, the answers are written in by the student as letters or numbers in a column at the right side of the page. Then it's merely a matter of checking off these answers against a "key" made out for each page.

In addition to the multiple-choice type, I usually try to have at least a question or two which must be answered in the student's own words. My children correct the number-answers, while Peg, with her training in Biology, is able to help me with the written answers. She started this originally as a help to me in my busy schedule with one hundred twenty-five high-school students, and after the first dozen papers there was no stopping her. The answers were just too interesting.

Some of the replies merely give a new angle to a word because of a brand-new way of spelling. This is the case with the title of this chapter. It came to me in answer to the request to give a biological description of man. What the student meant, of course, was that man is a *mammal*—he just forgot to add the final "l." But some of these misspellings turn out words that would surprise you.

For instance, in answer to the same question on the description of man, another student informed me that "when man eats, his food goes from his stomach into his small intentions."

Another student spelled intestines correctly, but decided that food gets "pasted on" through the digestive system. Actually, recalling the way I used to spoon babyfood off our small descendants' chins and smear it on again, perhaps he was right at that.

Other things I have learned about ourselves are that we have a gaul blotter, that our voice box shuts up when we do, that we breathe by means of lunks and that our blood is filled with red constables.

Also, in case you wondered, the four races of man are the mongreloid (Mongoloid), masculine, feminine and primitive. There is also a race known as the astronaut—one student's version, I suspect, of the Australoid.

On the subject of alcohol and narcotics, I also received a little new information. "The trouble with alcohol," in the words of one student, "is that it stimulates the brain to think more slowly." Another told me that it lowers the imbibitions. Still another suggested that it interfered with blood posture and may possibly give closeness of the liver. And when you take narcotics you may soon become an attic.

One of my favorite subjects in Biology is one which grows more important with our expanding population: the conservation of our natural resources. A youngster, in writing about forest fires, informed me that "the woods became hot and combusted." Another discussed the well-known observation that a predator dies off if it has no prey left to feed on. He put it this way: "It's like the lynx. This animal ate the rabbits so fast that it died of starvation."

My students always like to speculate as to why certain species have become extinct. "Extinct birds lay very few eggs," said one girl in a wondrous understatement. One of her classmates informed me that "extinct birds lay such a small number of eggs that reproduction can't keep pace with the rate of morality." Another proposed that animals in danger be protected from "foxes, wolves and other creditors." Still another suggested a cause of extinction as "hawks, owls, eagles and other birds with big fanged feet."

Once I asked my students to indicate what they thought to be the greatest single danger to the human species today. They mentioned atom bombs, delinquency, poverty and Communism. One, however, gave a better answer, misspelled, than I could have done by spelling correctly. "The greatest threat to human existence today," he wrote, "is the trouble with the human hearth."

Sometimes I give my students a list of terms to define. Peg enjoys correcting these because of the delightful way in which they get twisted. Among the ones we've jotted down are these:

> *Asphyxiation:* "When you indulge in too much carbon monoxide."
>
> *Degeneration:* "When you resemble your parents."
>
> *Degeneration:* "When you are not able to generate as you should."
>
> *Erosion:* "It makes a gully in the field. Then a cow comes along and steps in the gully. She breaks her leg, causing the farmer a considerable amount of damage."
>
> *Hypothesis:* "A scientific guest." (Guess)
>
> *Mammal:* "An animal that feeds its babies with mammy glands."
>
> *Pelorus Jack,* the famous harbor porpoise: "He was a porpus. Then he was shot. Then he was dead."
>
> *Reflex:* "This is like in the woodchuck. If it is shot at it may jump into the air several feet. When it comes down it is gone."
>
> *Smallpox:* "A disease that was perfected by Edward Jenner."
>
> *Ulcer:* "This is what happens when you're civilized."

My fellow teachers have their share of unexpected answers, too, so it's not peculiar to my field. Vivian Hutchins, who teaches the fifth grade, told me about a neat definition of democracy given by one of her students in class. "Democracy," said the ten-year-old, "is where the president doesn't tell us when to fight." Another student defined democracy as "when one president is the boss."

Peg once read a poem to her kindergarteners in which the word "sod" was mentioned. "Do any of you know what sod is?" she asked.

There was silence for a moment. Then a small boy raised his hand. "Mrs. Rood, I think a sod is something left over when you cut a board."

One day we were discussing the problem of borderline students in an informal faculty meeting. "I've got three or four pupils," said a ninth-grade teacher, "that are right on the fence between passing and failing. I hate to keep them back when they're so close to a passing grade. I know they could do better if they only tried. And yet, I don't know if I should send them along when they're so poorly prepared."

"You'd better ship them ahead," said the eighth-grade teacher, "because I'm sending you half a dozen more just like them."

Yet, just occasionally, some child sent on to a new grade justifies all the hope that the teacher has placed in him. I've had such a boy this past year. He suddenly caught fire around Thanksgiving. In every course he has gone from a near-failure to highest honors in the space between November and March. And, at this moment, he shows no sign of slowing down.

In fact the enthusiastic students present as much of a problem, in their way, as the ones who couldn't care less. When they suddenly wake up to what experimentation is all about, they're apt to be like the knight who rushed out of the castle, jumped on his horse, and galloped off in all directions. Sometimes the biggest challenge to me at the end of a wearisome day is to match the mood of a bubbling student who's been getting worked up about a particular project.

One girl put me in just such a spot when she appeared at the laboratory door after school one Friday.

"Mr. Rood, you said we really learn most when we do our own dissection, right?"

I assured her that this was the reason why each student takes apart eight or ten preserved specimens through the year.

"And you said we could bring in a dead mouse or squirrel or something that had been killed by a car or something?"

I told her she could bring in anything she wanted—within limits, of course.

"Well, Mr. Rood—is a turkey 'within limits?'"

I could just see the picture: twenty or thirty pounds of valuable gobbler, spirited off her father's farm before dawn and hauled to school in the back of the bus. Feathers all over the lab, three hours' work with a scalpel and forceps, and the end result a big pan of turkey hash—uncooked.

"Well now, Susie," I began, "that's a pretty big order. Everything we've dissected in the lab has been small. You know, clams and earthworms and grasshoppers and pickled frogs." Then as a happy afterthought I added: "And is this all right with your folks?"

"Oh, my folks don't know about it. Yet."

"Good. I mean—good girl to ask them. Let me know what they say. All right?"

And, luckily, this is as far as it went. A week or so later I chanced upon a pigeon on the sidewalk in Vergennes. It had apparently flown into a store window and broken its neck. I quickly gave it to Susie, and she gracefully accepted the substitute. But one of these days I'm not going to be so fortunate.

Susie's enthusiasm, however, paled beside that of an exuberant sophomore I had last year. I'd obtained a few seeds of rye which had been exposed to radioactivity at Dartmouth College. Radioactivity is apt to produce changes in the developing embryo. These changes may show up in the new plant as oversized leaves, stunted growth, short stems, and so on. We planted the seeds, and Charles was enthralled by the huge size of one of the plants.

"Wouldn't it be possible to grow rye as big as corn plants by exposing the seeds to radioactivity?"

I told him it could happen, but that radioactivity might also produce stunted plants.

"But can't scientists control the result of exposure to radiation?"

he wondered. "You know, give a little dose to make stunted plants and a big dose to make huge plants?"

I was out of my depth there, but I was able to tell him I'd heard that one of the problems was that control of the results was not possible. It needed further study.

"Oh. Well, why can't we set up a little radiation laboratory?"

I pointed out that such a lab would break the whole school's budget. Nevertheless I sent him to the physics teacher and helped him write a letter to the Atomic Energy Commission for more information. And he's currently raising more rye seeds to find out what he'll get this time. So as yet we don't have any "hot" rooms at the high school, and we don't have to monitor each other with dosimeters and geiger counters at closing bell each day.

Occasionally my family has to absorb the overflow of enthusiasm when student zeal gets a little out of hand. This was the case last year on the day before Easter vacation. Donald Codling met me at the door of my room in the morning with a cloth satchel.

"Mr. Rood, you said if we found anything unusual to bring it in, didn't you?"

I nodded.

"Even snakes?"

"Sure. Do you have a snake in that bag?"

"Well, it's not exactly *a* snake, Mr. Rood," he said as he opened the bag. "It's thirty-two of 'em."

"*Thirty-two?*"

"Yep. Found 'em under a lumber pile. Hibernating, I guess. They were cold and sleepy. So I brought them to you for your lab."

We took them into the laboratory and opened the bag. They were harmless garter snakes—still stupefied from their long sleep, but I knew they'd soon revive.

"Look, Donald. Take them out to the car. Put the bag right in the back seat. They'll stay cool there all day. I'll take them home with me over vacation, if you can spare that satchel."

136

"MAN IS A MAMMA"

Thus it was that Peg and I played nursemaid during vacation to thirty-two garter snakes. My children went out and dug earthworms from the newly thawed earth to feed them. The townspeople pointed to their heads significantly when they heard about our latest guests. And as soon as school was again in session, I gave my students an impromptu exercise on a laboratory animal I hadn't expected to have.

There's a sequel to this story. After we'd studied them, a number of the students asked me if they could take one home as a pet. I weeded out those youngsters who were merely curious or who had cats at home—cats and snakes don't get along—and finally presented fifteen students with a snake apiece.

I've never bothered to ask their parents how things went at home. But later, when we had an Open House at the school one night, several of the parents pointedly said, "So *you're* Mr. Rood. I've been wanting to *meet* you."

I wonder if they have that homicidal gleam in their eyes when they speak to the other teachers?

And so the Donalds and the Charleses and the Susies add their own brand of problems to a teacher's life. As I try to channel their eagerness along productive, rewarding and challenging lines, I keep wondering if I'm doing all I can for them—if there's some stone I've left unturned. Then I remember a comment made by a friend upon his retirement from the teaching profession: "A good student will learn in spite of his teacher."

One year at graduation time I served as an usher. It was my duty to hand out programs at the door and give a welcoming smile to parents and guests. Several temporary workers were also employed to assist parking, traffic control, lighting, and so on. Two of them peered in at the door as the ceremonies were in progress.

"What's going on, Walt?" they asked a third worker who had been standing with me just outside the door of the auditorium.

"Oh, they're talking. First they had a talk from the valleydictorian. Now they're having a talk from the sally-dictorian."

"Holy smokes! When's it ever going to end?"

"I don't know. Never, if you ask me."

I looked at those gowned figures on the stage. I thought of the reams of paper, the hours of study, the armloads of homework that parents and teachers and students had shared alike. I thought of Peg and Janice and Tom and Alison and Roger—all armed with red pencils and seated with me around a bunch of tests on the big kitchen table.

Then I considered Walt's answer as to when it all would come to an end: "Never, if you ask me."

I hope he's right.

CHAPTER TWELVE

Busman's Holiday

THE NEW JERSEY flats stretched before us. The smell of salt marsh, factory smoke and auto exhaust blew in the open windows of our micro-bus station wagon. The noise of passing cars and the singing of the tires beat constantly in our ears. But we didn't care. We were headed for the Chincoteague pony roundup.

"Chincoteague," the travel folder had read, "is Virginia's largest island. It is at the end of the Delmarva Peninsula. Each year it's the scene of the most famous wild-west show in the East— the wild pony roundup."

I had heard about the annual "pony swim" years ago when I was working with Doc Pyenson in extension work on Long Island. Doc had told me of an oversized sand dune called Assateague which is located just offshore of Chincoteague. It seems that a ship carrying horses was once wrecked there. Or perhaps it merely let the horses off and never came back for them. At any rate, they were still there, apparently stunted in growth because of their harsh surroundings. They were supposed to be about mid-way in size between a Shetland pony and a small horse. However, they weren't as chunky as some ponies, but well formed, wiry and tough.

"They round the ponies up on Assateague Island and swim them across the channel to Chincoteague?" I asked.

He indicated that this was right—that the Chincoteague firemen had the pony swim the last Wednesday and Thursday in July. This was in connection with a huge carnival for more than a week before the swim. After this, the pony foals were auctioned off.

"Good heavens!" I said. "Don't tell me the young ponies have to swim the channel too!"

Doc laughed. "I wouldn't know. Why don't you go down there and see for yourself?"

So here we were some twelve years later, out to see for ourselves. I had no summer school to attend this year. My last writing assignment had recently been finished. We left the dog with neighbors and headed south from our home in Vermont.

I'd been introduced by mail to Warren Conant, Chincoteague's postmaster, telling him we were planning to camp at the municipal campground, "but we'd like to get some suggestions about where to go and what to see while we were there."

"We'll be looking for you," he wrote back. "Come early and stay late. Look me up as soon as you get into town."

"Town," during the last week of the Firemen's Carnival, proved to combine the gaiety of Coney Island with the charm of Cape Cod. We drove along the main street past camera shops, drugstores and gift shops, all doing a whacking vacation business. Girls in shorts mingled with fishermen in rubber boots, and traffic crawled along in low gear. As we came to the edge of town we passed the institution that fostered much of it—the carnival, fairly quiet now during the day but shortly to blaze at sunset.

Everywhere we saw Chincoteague ponies. Many were nearly as big as Chichi, our own little half-Morgan mare back in Vermont. They carried children and their parents up and down the street. Some of them were penned in front-yard corrals for the occasion. "For sale: Genuine Chincoteague Ponies," Alison read excitedly.

"Oh, Daddy—couldn't we buy one and have it shipped back home?"

I was just about to answer her when Roger cut in at the top of his voice. "Stop, Daddy! Stop! I saw a sign about Misty!"

The children had read Marguerite Henry's charming book, *Misty of Chincoteague,* and knew every one of Wesley Dennis's illustrations by heart. They'd been looking for signs of the famous little pony ever since we had arrived. Now, as I stopped in the street, Roger craned his neck out the window.

I looked in the mirror. A line of cars a block long was behind me. "Better walk back and see what it says, Roger," I decided, pulling over to the curb. The words were scarcely out of my mouth before he and Alison had burst out of the door and gone running down the sidewalk.

They came back in an instant. "Beebe Ranch," Alison directed breathlessly. "Down this street and turn left."

In a few minutes we drew up to the Beebe Ranch. We parked in front of a little gift shop which fronted on a stable. The children took out their pocketbooks and counted out the necessary coins. Then, having paid their admission, they walked reverently into Misty's presence.

Peg and I took a brief look at the plucky little mare who'd once made the channel swim herself and, according to the story, had nearly drowned in the crossing. We admired her golden coat and silvery mane, and then went back outside.

We were joined shortly by our two starry-eyed youngsters. "Oh, Alison, isn't she pretty?" Roger asked.

"She's more than that, Roger. She's beautiful!"

Peg smiled. "And now, kids, would you let your father drive to the campground before all the tentsites are taken?"

We bumped over a short sandy road to a grassy area with a few trees. It curved around a beach that was half sand, half rocks. CAMPGROUND, announced a sign and, as if to prove it, there were three or four tents pitched near the water's edge.

After we'd set up camp we went back to town to meet Warren

141

Conant. I expressed surprise that the campground was so empty, but he assured me I'd soon have more than enough company.

"Today's only Monday. You wait 'til tomorrow—the day before the pony swim. It'll be so crowded that you'll think half the town's moved in on you."

I shrugged doubtfully, but it later became evident that he'd actually understated the case. Other campers began to unload almost at once, and soon it looked as if the gypsies had arrived. So great is the charm of this leisurely village and so strong is the lure of "pony penning," as it is called, that many of the states of the Union were represented in the license plates of the cars.

We felt lucky in having arrived before the mob and establishing our territory first. It was situated so that we could drive our micro-bus right next to our tent, while latecomers were obliged to park out in the road. But our advantage was short-lived. One time, after having been away for a couple of hours, we returned to find a small umbrella tent in our parking spot. From then on we parked with the other cars, and so, according to Peg, got a preview of what the population explosion is going to be like.

We explored the little village on foot and by auto. Warren Conant, his impish grin far from matching his white hair, introduced us to "everybody I can think of" on the island. We went for a half-day ride in a beach buggy over the sands of the Chincoteague National Wildlife Refuge. We enjoyed steamed crabs with Warren and Pauline Conant, picked some of the famous Chincoteague oysters off the mud-flats, and skimmed out to the Conant camp on an island in the middle of Chincoteague Bay.

This last trip reminded me of a downwind landing I once made in my days as an Air Force cadet with the wind at my back—all bumps and plenty of speed. It was made in what Warren called a Chincoteague Scow: a sloping-bottomed boat of such shallow draft that it looked as if it could navigate a golf course on a muddy day.

Finally the big morning came. Driven to a point of land on

142

Assateague by "gumboot cowboys"—horseback riders whose daily activities usually involved fishing, clamming or other marine activity—the two hundred or so stallions, mares and colts grazed with apparent calm on the salt-grass. Opposite them, somewhat less than a quarter-mile away on the Chincoteague shore, were several thousand tourists, vacationists, townspeople, photographers, writers and reporters.

Between these two groups stretched the channel crammed with scores of boats. These ranged from our craft, a scow belonging to Warren's friend known as "Cigar" after the stogie he bore, to sizable yachts and a Coast Guard boat. There was even a red Ford V-8 convertible, mounted on a hull and fitted for a seafaring life. Over this assemblage hovered the Coast Guard boat like a mother hen, keeping her "chicks" out of the main portion of the channel where the ponies were to swim.

All morning the tide had been running in from the ocean like a river. Now, by about 11 A.M., it was almost at the flood. "Low tide is better," Cigar stated, "but it comes at the wrong time of day just now. So the boys are waiting for just the right moment at high tide. Then they'll swim the ponies across before the water turns and runs out again."

Suddenly there was a commotion on the opposite shore. The waiting cowboys spurred their horses. They shouted and whistled and drove the ponies to the water's edge. Here the herd hesitated, but the cowboys urged them on. They slapped the water with reins and ropes while the cowboys in the rear crowded the herd from behind.

Then the ponies took to the water. I had heard about the pony swim in several books, but the one thing that immediately impressed me had not been mentioned in any of them. This was the sound of some two hundred horses calling, neighing, whinnying to each other as they stretched their necks toward the opposite shore. It was a sound we shall never forget.

We watched the pony foals through our binoculars. Some of the little fellows laid their heads on their mothers' rumps to keep their noses out of the water. Their high-pitched little voices sounded over the calls of their parents as they flailed their tiny hoofs in the strange medium.

Finally they made it to our shore. The tide was stronger than the cowboy-firemen had calculated, and the herd had drifted downstream a few hundred feet from where they were supposed to land. Men, women and children melted away before them as the ponies found the ground and pulled themselves out of the water. Dripping and neighing, they were driven to a waiting corral. There they quickly re-formed into family groups, each stallion claiming his dozen or so mares and their foals.

The next day found us with thousands of others at the pony auction. The ponies, being wild creatures rounded up by the firemen, had become the latter's property. Now their foals—or to use proper Chincoteague parlance, colts—were singled out and held in a little corral. Each "mahr" (mare) colt or "hoss" (horse) colt came to the block in its turn. There one or more husky firemen held the wild little creature as best they could while it was bid off. Apparently even though they were only about two months old, they were old enough for instant weaning to grain and grass, as this had been happening to colts after the auctions for years.

"Fifty-five, who'll make it sixty? Fifty-five, who'll make it sixty? . . . Sixty, who says sixty-five?" the auctioneer chanted as the "hoss" and "mahr" colts were presented for sale.

Some of the buyers were obviously outfitted for just this occasion. There were horse-trailers from Kentucky, and fancy vans from Pennsylvania. There were people in pickup trucks and delivery wagons.

Other buyers were people who came to look and ended up owning one of the charming little colts. An auction will do that to you. A woman from Baltimore was among this group. "Eighty!" she shouted in a fit of enthusiasm at my side as a fine little brown-and-white colt kicked and struggled in his captor's arms.

The auctioneer waited for other bids. "Are you all done at eighty?" he called. Then he pointed to her. "Lady, you done bought yourself a hoss."

She clapped her hand to her forehead. "Oh, no! Where will I put him when I get home?" Then, happily: "But won't Lester be surprised?"

Several of the firemen looked on as she bargained with the owner of a pickup truck for transportation. Then one of the men turned to me. "There's a divorce case if I ever saw one," he grinned.

There were plenty of other impulse-buyers. And among them was a family in a micro-bus from Vermont.

Roger and Alison had watched one little colt after another come up for sale. Finally Roger came over to me and pressed his pocket-book into my hand.

"Alison's money is back in the car," he said. "But here's all my money. Dad, could you put enough with it to buy us a pony?"

At this moment, I knew, there was nothing short of life itself that was more precious to my children. We didn't have a horse-trailer and we surely didn't have the money. But we were at Chincoteague and this was the pony auction.

"All right, Roger. Pick out the one you want."

"Golly, Dad. Golly. How much can we spend?"

"See if you can get one for about fifty-five dollars."

The hoss colts had been going for anywhere from fifty to seventy-five dollars, while the mahrs had averaged somewhat higher. I watched, happy as only a father can feel when he is able to give his son something he knows the youngster wants badly.

Carefully Roger made his choice. It was one of the smallest colts yet to be offered. Light brown with a straight little back and legs, he kicked and struggled in silence as the auctioneer's helper tried to keep him still.

"Who'll go fifty dollars to start it off?" the auctioneer asked.

"Forty!" shouted Roger.

"Forty I've got. Who'll make it forty-five?"

Someone on the other side of the crowd bid forty-five. Roger bid fifty. Then it went up in dollar amounts until the opposition had bid fifty-five.

Roger looked at me in despair. "Oh, Dad, what do I do now?"

A man at my side in a ten-gallon hat winked at me. "Surely you could spare the boy another dollar."

"All right, Roger. Tell him fifty-six."

"Fifty-six!" shouted Roger.

But the opposition was still with us. "Fifty-seven!"

My big-hatted friend turned to me again. "Now here's how to get your pony. Tell the boy to go all the way to sixty."

I nodded. Roger took a good hitch on his lungs. "Sixty!" he shouted in his best eleven-year-old, hoss-tradin' voice.

The auctioneer turned and looked full at my son. "Boy," he said gently, "this here's a fine hoss for a fella just your size. And he's yours for sixty dollars."

Alison had been watching, flabbergasted. Now she rushed over. "Daddy, is it true? It is really true? Is he ours?"

Peg cleared her throat beside me. I'd almost forgotten her. "Yes, Alison, he's ours. Now all your father's got to do is get him back to Vermont."

We bought a little halter with our now sadly depleted cash, and managed to slip it over the tiny colt's nose. "What'll we call him, Dad?" asked Roger.

"I don't know. What's a good name?"

"How about 'Little Fellow'?"

And so Little Fellow joined our family.

The problem now was to see if we could get him from Virginia to Vermont. I measured him with my arms and then calculated how he'd fit in our bus-wagon. We'd already taken out the middle seat to make room for camping equipment, and just maybe . . .

So I drove to the postoffice. "Guess what?" I asked Warren. But he didn't have to guess.

"You bought a pony."

"Yep. Cute little feller. The description of him on the sales slip says 'mouse brown.' Got any packing lumber around the place?"

So we sawed and nailed. In a couple of hours we had a sturdy stall built. It was four feet long, thirty inches wide, and three feet high—a perfect fit for our tiny guest.

The children practiced leading the little colt around the campground. At first he protested and dragged them around a bit "just to show us he's got spunk," Roger told us between puffs. But soon he followed them in fine shape as if he'd been used to people all the two months of his life.

Finally came the time to put Little Fellow in the car. We'd fixed one end of his crate so it could be put up as a ramp for him. Roger went into the micro-bus coaxing and gently pulling the lead rope, and I urged him from the rear. Then, with a leap, he disdained the ramp and jumped into the car so fast he bumped his nose on the opposite window.

A small crowd had gathered to watch the proceedings. They cheered and whistled as we drove away. On the way out of town we stopped to show Warren how nicely his handiwork fitted the occasion. "I have a parting gift," he winked as he led us out to the side of the building. There was a little bale of hay.

"Chincoteague hay," he said. "Just for Little Fellow, so he won't get homesick. It's what he's used to. It will go on the floor by his crate. I've already measured it."

So, with a pailful of grain from the Beebe Ranch and Warren's going-away present, we left the island with our four-legged passenger.

From the first he was a perfect traveler. Newspapers and straw beneath him made a soft, absorbent bed. He tried to go to sleep, but with every jolt he'd wake up. Then he'd glance around at his new family with a little nicker of recognition and slowly doze off again.

All along the way we were the subject of much scrutiny, double-takes and near-collisions as drivers and passengers in other cars contemplated the unlikely spectacle of a horse in a station wagon. One car which passed us slowed down when it got in front until we were forced to pass it in turn. Then it pulled abreast of us on a straight stretch. In the car we could see a man and a woman. The woman was taking pictures of us with her home-movie camera. So somewhere, in somebody's collection, Little Fellow is in the movies.

On the way back we camped overnight along Virginia's Skyline Drive. We arrived at the campground quite late in the evening and found just one tentsite left. This was one adjacent to the rest rooms.

It was a warm, clear night, so we just spread out the sleeping bags without bothering to put up the tent. To our chagrin, we discovered that we were sleeping just a few feet from a shortcut to the rest rooms. It looked as if we'd have people wandering through our camp all night.

I dozed off once or twice, waking when I heard people walking past. Then I heard Roger get up, but I was too sleepy to see what he was doing. After that, though, it seemed as if the campsite became unusually peaceful, and we fell asleep.

Next morning I understood the reason for the sudden calm. Roger had quietly untied Little Fellow from a tree where he'd been standing. Then he'd tied him right in the middle of the path. Would-be visitors to the rest rooms, coming upon a dark creature standing in the path, quickly retraced their steps and—I trust—visited the rest rooms via another route.

We continued north with our pony. He occasioned a few raised eyebrows at toll bridges when the attendants tried to decide if he was a passenger or not. He panicked a little dog at a gas station when we suddenly let him out on a parking ramp. We discovered that he'd whinny if Roger left the car, so at more than one picnic area we'd have him whinny. Then we'd innocently stare into space while the other people at nearby tables would try to figure out where the horse must be.

We let our little hoss colt out every fifty miles or so for a rest-stop and managed to keep him as fresh and clean as his native sand dunes all the way home. When we added up the miles we'd traveled with him on our leisurely side-jaunts through the Shenandoah National Park, we discovered he'd been with us in the car for five days and fifteen hundred miles.

At this writing in March, Little Fellow is about ten months old. Now he weighs perhaps a hundred fifty pounds and stands forty inches high. He grew a thick coat of hair to protect him against the Vermont winter, and spent half the time outdoors—though the barn door was open for shelter if he wanted it.

He's fine company for Chichi and Beauty, our two mares. But not long ago Alison said to me:

"Daddy, what Little Fellow needs is not a couple of great big horses but a little mahr colt."

So possibly we'll be heading south for another busman's holiday. After all, we've not had a horse in the micro-bus since last August.

Besides, as Warren Conant says, "once you get that Chincoteague sand in your shoes, you'll come back again."

And that, undoubtedly, is a fact.

CHAPTER THIRTEEN

Full Circle

THREE FRIENDS came to visit shortly after we'd moved to Vermont. I'd had them as pupils when I was at the Institute down on Long Island. Now they'd located jobs in upstate New York, and had come across Lake Champlain for the weekend to see me.

I took them to a number of spots on our hundred acres. I showed them the spreading view of the Green Mountains from our back pasture. I took them up on the north knoll where I hope some day to build that little house for Peg and me so we can turn the farmhouse over to visiting descendants when they're grown. I explained how our bridge serves as our doorbell, and had Janice ride her bicycle across its loose planks as a demonstration.

While I had them on the tour, Peg had blended milk, vanilla, sugar and some of Daisy's best cream into a thick, sweet mixture. I poured it into a hand-cranked freezer, and made them a half-gallon of ice cream. Then we scooped it out into dishes and ladled our own maple syrup over it, with a few crushed Vermont hickory nuts on top.

As we enjoyed our Green Mountain sundae, Peg and I tried to help them picture what it must be like at other times of the year. We described the flaming autumn foliage, and told them of woods deep with snow. We described the spring break-up of ice on the rivers and even admitted to a fifth season in Vermont—"mud season," as Howard Masterson, our road commissioner says, "when these gravel roads around here thaw out so they'll barely float a car."

Finally it came time for our visitors to leave. Two of them climbed into the car, but the third stood for a moment with his hand on the door. "There's just one thing that puzzles me," he said as he gazed slowly around at the Vermont countryside.

"What's that?" I asked.

"Well, I've always wanted a place of my own in Vermont. But until today I never realized how wild the country can be. We can't see a single house in any direction from where we're standing now. Sure the leaves are pretty and the flowers are beautiful and the view from your front lawn is like a picture postcard. But what can you ever *do* here?"

As I recall, I gave him a lame answer about the joy of making your own entertainment instead of having it served to you by someone else.

I'm sure he drove away unconvinced. "The trouble is," he said, "even if I wanted to learn to enjoy the land as you and your family do, I wouldn't know how to start."

This parting comment intrigued me. As I thought it over after they were gone, I realized it was almost a challenge. Just saying "Oh, you'll learn to enjoy the outdoors" is hardly good enough. It's like a tennis star I saw years ago who played a brilliant series of games and won the match.

"Practice, my boy. Practice and more practice," he'd said when I asked him for advice on becoming a tennis player. Yet this was little help to a boy who didn't know the first thing about the game—who neither knew *what* to practice nor how to go about it.

Now I recognized the same quest for information in my friend. "How do I start?" was really what I'd meant to ask the tennis player. My friend left before I could help him, but

151

perhaps I could help others. So, when guests come for more than a quick chat, we're often apt to get off on the subject of which we're so fond: the land around us and how to enjoy it.

We begin by urging our would-be naturalist to slow down. Otherwise he'll go right past lots of things without seeing them— like a hunter friend of mine who goes clumping through the woods and then complains that all he ever sees is the flashing white tails of fleeing deer. And of course the story is the same for anybody: if you try to cover the most ground in the least time you're doing little more than running an obstacle course. The wild animals hear you coming and have disappeared before you could possibly see them.

I remember reading somewhere that a sitting man is far less formidable than a standing man. That's why Peg and I like to go out in the woods and just sit quietly. We sometimes sit back to back, so we can see in all directions.

When we first sit down, the woods seem quiet and uninhabited. Soon, however, little noises begin. The leaves stir. A piece of bark flutters down from some creature in the trees above. Little by little the forest forgets the intrusion of man.

One August evening I sat down with my back to a mossy log. The day was still warm and I became drowsy. I lay down next to the log and curled up for a nap.

As I slept, a strange sensation came into my consciousness. It was as if something was tapping gently on my leg. Finally, realizing that it was not a dream, I slowly opened my eyes. There were three of the daintiest creatures in the woods using me for a springboard.

Orange-brown with slender tails nearly six inches long, my tiny visitors were woodland jumping mice. Running along the log, they hopped off onto me and then into the leaves like playful frogs. Off they'd go, covering several feet at a bound. In a minute they'd be back to repeat the game.

I'd seen a few jumping mice before, but only when I'd surprised them by overturning a log or startling one out of its little sheltered nest. Never had I seen them at play—certainly never before had I been used as a Trampoline, either.

Another time I was rewarded for being still was in our spruce woods in the midst of winter. It was a cold moonlit night, and the trunks of the trees stood out in contrast against the snowy background. The crunching of my boots on the snow was the only sound there seemed to be in the entire world.

A tree near me cracked with a sharp report, splitting with the cold. The sound startled me so that I stopped. Realizing what it was, I stood there listening for other trees.

Then a motion back down the trail caught my attention in the moonlight. I could see a shadowy white figure hopping along in my tracks. As it drew closer I saw that it was about the size of a slender chipmunk, but somewhat longer.

Three or four of my footsteps away, the figure paused. It had been nosing each track in succession; now it raised its head and looked at me. It was a weasel in its royal winter coat of ermine. Following my tracks out of curiosity, it had been going nearly as fast as I had been walking. Had I not stopped, I would never have seen it. And, in a flash, it turned and fled.

Very few of our winter walks are uneventful. Two months ago Janice and I went along the brook that comes out of our woods and flows into the pasture. The water was domed over with ice, beneath which we could hear the gurgle of hidden rapids. Out of curiosity we broke through the ice and turned over a large flat stone. There in the frigid water were three salamanders and a couple of crane-fly larvae—the latter to turn into those long-legged harmless flies that look like great mosquitoes in summer. Yet, on the surface, the brook would have seemed completely lifeless.

Next we pulled the bark off an old birch stump and looked beneath it. There were spiders and beetles and the cocoon of a moth—waiting for spring to come. So even in the dead of winter, life can be found if you look for it.

When we used to fish in Long Island Sound, we'd keep our eyes open for a gathering of gulls. This almost always indicated the presence of fish. In the same way, the behavior of a flock of jays or crows or pigeons may give a clue that something unusual is going on. One day I was driving over a little country road with a friend when he noticed a flock of pigeons circling over a field.

I slowed the car for a better look. The funnel of flying pigeons was poised above a few of their number which were on the ground. They were cautiously approaching some object lying in the short grass.

"Wonder what that lump of stuff could be in the field? Stop the car, Ron."

No sooner had I stopped than the "lump of stuff" came to life. There was a flurry of pigeons as the object jumped to its feet and made a grab at the nearest bird. Missing, it raced for the woods— a full-grown red fox. It had been playing 'possum right out in the open in hopes of getting a pigeon. I had upset its little scheme by stopping the car instead of driving right by. Wise in the ways of hunters, it had fled just in case we planned to send a bullet after it.

If we'd been speeding by, we never would have noticed the little drama. As it was, some lucky pigeon had a reprieve, while some little foxes may have gone hungry a little longer.

It's surprising how little we can see sometimes, at highway speeds. Half hypnotized by the ribbon of road as it unwinds before us, we're scarcely likely to glance to right or left. One time we had a soft tire along the New York State Thruway. As I pulled off the side of the road, I noticed a woodchuck feeding in the short grass along the shoulder. He scuttled for cover at the sight of this juggernaut which had deserted the pavement and was bearing down on him.

"That's six of them for my side," said Alison, after we'd safely stopped.

"Six what?" Peg asked.

"Woodchucks. Roger and I have been counting them ever since

154

we got on at Albany. He's got four on the left of the road and I've got six on the right."

We'd gone about thirty miles. That meant a woodchuck for every three miles, not counting the ones they hadn't seen. As for me, I had noticed just two—plus a dead one right in the middle of the road that neither of them had seen!

Last fall I was asked to go along on a Boy Scout hike as an advisor. "Use your smell and taste, as well as ears, eyes and touch," I told a small companion who was walking beside me. As I said it, I realized I was echoing those same words said to me a generation ago by Mr. Lake as I trotted along beside him on a woodland trail. And thus the wheel has come full circle.

I often urge my friends to discover what I have discovered— that woods and swamps and fields all have their distinctive sounds and smells as well as appearance. You can find this for yourself by closing your eyes as you ride in a car with the windows open. After a while you'll be able to guess what kind of country you're passing through. Or close your eyes as you relax somewhere out in the open. As you listen and sniff, the lands takes on new personality.

As you walk through the country, break the ends of twigs and you'll discover that many trees have their own distinctive odor and taste. Peach and cherry smell like almond. Some birches taste like wintergreen, and sassafras has the flavor of root beer. Maple twigs are reminiscent of syrup. Globs of gum which have oozed from the bark of spruce trees were used by settlers as chewing gum. Scarlet sumac berries—hardly to be confused with poison sumac with its white berries—have a sour lemon taste. These, too, the settlers used, crushing them in water and then straining and sweetening the infusion like lemonade.

I also encourage using the sense of touch to help "collect" plants by learning their peculiarities. The horsetail plant is a slender green stalk, apparently without leaves, growing along roadsides and ditches. Rubbed between the fingers, it gives a dry scratching feel, due to the silica in its tissues. This indicates its second name: "scour-

155

ing rush," so called by the settlers before the days of steel wool.

A plant can be tabbed as a member of the mint family by rolling it between the fingers. Its square stem is readily recognized in addition to its minty aroma. The grasslike sedges of swampy land are usually easy to identify by a three-cornered feel to the stem. Some leaves feel waxy, others sticky, and so on.

It's this thrill of discovery—using your eyes, your ears, your senses of smell and taste and touch—that helps me impress on my friends that there *is* something to do here.

We need plenty of help, ourselves, in our ramblings over our hundred acres. Sight and hearing and the other senses are not enough. There are scores of mushrooms, scores of birds, mammals, fish, flowers, trees, amphibians, reptiles, rocks, minerals, insects: far more than any one mind could encompass. So we use the services of our friends who may be informed on certain subjects, whenever we can wheedle their help. In a few weeks Mrs. Henrietta Field, an accomplished botanist who lives in a neighboring town, is going to join me in labeling some hundred trees and shrubs along a nature trail I've made in our woods.

And when we lack such first-hand assistance, we fall back on field guidebooks in the various subjects to help us—just as any beginner can, for the guides are written for the layman.

The most important "sense" we have in our collecting, however, is that of imagination. It is imagination that allows us to appreciate the thrush at twilight. The owl hears it, too, but considers it only as a means to a possible dinner. Our sense of smell tells us a skunk has passed by on a spring evening, but it takes the human mind to conjure up a picture of what might have happened.

The Indians, of course, were masters at deciphering the tale inherent in a few tracks or a broken twig. They could piece together a story where a less observant person would not even know anything had happened. Therefore the mind of the Indian often endowed wild animals with spirits akin to his own. "Wild brothers," he would say of the creatures around him. Sometimes he

156

would offer a little prayer of apology to the spirit of the deer before he sent the arrow to its mark.

On more than one occasion the phrase "wild brother" has come to me in some of my experiences with animals over the years. These have been when some wild creature has shown an amazing and sudden trust in man.

One occasion stands out vividly in my memory. It concerns an experience my brother and I had on our parents' farm in Connecticut.

Jimmy and I had been walking along the edge of our brook, looking for skunk cabbages. These odorous blooms, cousins of the calla lily and jack-in-the-pulpit, were among the first plants to appear in the spring. In fact it was only January, and already we'd spotted several of the purple-brown hoods poking up through the mud and slush of the Connecticut marshland.

We were looking for skunk cabbages, yes. But not skunks. Yet we came across a skunk, caught by his front foot in a steel trap.

Dad had never allowed trappers on his land since the time he'd had to dig a red fox out of a rocky den. The fox had been caught in a trap somewhere, and had dragged the trap, chain and all, back to his home. There his desperate whines were audible many feet away from the den entrance. Dad spent nearly two days getting him out. "By thunder," he said after he'd released the fox, "no more traps on my land—ever!"

Nevertheless here was a trap. Perhaps set for muskrats, it had caught a skunk as he puddled along the water's edge. Probably he'd been looking in the debris for edibles during this thaw that had interrupted his winter nap.

I inched my way toward the skunk. "Watch out," breathed Jimmy, who had been instructed to stay well out of the way. "You're going to be sorry, Ronny."

But I kept right on. Talking soothingly to the animal, I reached forward until my hand closed around the trap. He had pulled as far away from me as the chain would let him, and now he surveyed me with his little black eyes. The trap had caught him just above the wrist, but the bones didn't seem to be broken.

Reaching forward with the other hand, I grasped both sides of the trap. The skunk remained perfectly still, watching. Slowly I pressed down with both hands, releasing the spring catch.

Suddenly the imprisoned leg came free. The skunk had been pulling hard; now he tumbled backward in a heap. Righting himself, he stood there for a moment in his new freedom. He held the injured leg up off the ground and looked at us for a long time. No more eloquent thanks could have been expressed if he'd been able to talk.

Then, unhurriedly, he turned and hobbled away.

This incident happened when we were children. I wasn't surprised at the outcome at the time, for, in my small-boy way, I figured that the skunk understood what I was trying to do. And since then I've seen plenty of evidence of the special behavior animals show toward man when they're in trouble.

One of the most striking cases was told to us by a National Park Ranger three years ago. It concerned a mother bear, her cub, and a human being—a situation bound to be fraught with danger.

We were camped at Yellowstone, watching a mother and her two cubs make the rounds of the garbage pails near the campsites. "Aren't they cute?" said Alison. "Just like two little teddy bears and their mother."

"Yes," I agreed, "but you try to interfere with one of those teddies, and see how cute they are. Mother bear would knock you into the middle of next week." I looked to the ranger for confirmation.

"Well, you're right—usually," he agreed. "But I know of one man who did it and got away with it." And he told us the following story.

A couple of campers were setting up their tent one evening when the husband heard a commotion at an empty site near by. He looked over and saw that a small cub had poked its head down into a tin can, and couldn't get it back out again. The frenzied creature was running wildly, knocking into trees and slamming into rocks and howling for all it was worth, trying to escape from the can. Meanwhile the mother bear was running along a short distance away, completely at a loss about what to do.

Finally the cub banged its way over toward the man. The camper had never been around bears much, so he didn't know enough to be scared. He just stood there while the little fellow came within fifteen feet of him. Then he got the idea to help. Handing his wife the hatchet for protection, he walked right up to the cub——

"And bigosh," the ranger concluded, "if he didn't yank the can right off that cub's head while the old lady bear just stood and watched."

Thinking of the skunk I'd rescued as a boy, I could imagine how such a foolhardy act could have been carried through without mishap. I recalled, too, the way the surprising gentleness of our big loon with his murderous beak had exemplified the trust that wild creatures sometimes place in human beings.

Even so unlikely a subject as a porcupine may throw himself on human mercy when everything fails. One May day our little town of Lincoln sprang to life as the fire whistle blew at the local mill. Vermont woods don't often catch fire, for the Green Mountains are well named, but this day high winds and a long dry spell combined to carry a trash fire into the forest.

By the time the blaze had been brought under control, about sixty acres of woodland had been burned. Nothing green remained: the fire had done a thorough job.

One of the workers was beating out the last sparks with a shovel when he heard a whimpering cry. Looking down, he saw a tiny porcupine, running toward him in the hot ashes, crying as sparks touched his little feet. Orphaned in the fire, he turned to the one living thing he saw—even if it was Man, the arch-enemy.

The worker later brought me the little quill-pig. The game wardens didn't want him, so we finally ended up with him ourselves. We named him Pokey and kept him around the place for a year. Finally we released him in our woods. Again the trust of a wild animal in distress had been rewarded.

A friend of mine who raises bees told of an instance where a mother mouse put her fate completely in his hands. "Every winter the darned mice get into my beehives," Charles Weigold said. "They chew the wax, spoil the honey, and sometimes build a nest. The bees often sting a mouse to death and plaster it up with pro-polis, or bee-glue, because it's too big to carry out. But mice in a beehive can sure wreck things.

"One spring I was cleaning out my hives. I came to a big cluster of leaves and downy material at the bottom of a hive. It was the nest of a white-footed mouse. As I yanked it apart, three little pink mice fell out. They were so tiny and naked they looked like little grubs. Then the mother ran out with a fourth one in her mouth.

"She ran over into the bushes and dropped the baby there. I held the other three in my hand.

"'If you want 'em, you've got to come and get 'em,' I told her. Of course she couldn't understand me, but she came back to where the babies were squeaking in my hand. Then she sat up like a little squirrel and put her front paws together as if she were begging. So I opened my hand and let her take her little ones —one at a time."

Mr. Weigold looked at me a little sheepishly. "I suppose I should have killed them all on the spot," he said, "after all the trouble they caused. But when a little mouse like that shows that much courage, you have to be pretty low-down not to help her out."

Harold Blaisdell, whose books on fishing have lightened my heart—and, occasionally, weighted my creel—once told our Forest and Field Club of a friendship that he struck up with a raccoon.

He and his son were fishing at the shore of a little lake. The only thing they were getting were small sunfish, and they were about to give up in disgust when the boy happened to notice a raccoon poking along the shore some distance away.

They watched him quietly as he worked his way closer. When he was just a few feet away, they flipped him one of the sunfish. The 'coon recoiled in surprise, but soon returned to the flopping fish. Then he proceeded to eat it.

"This gave us an idea," Mr. Blaisdell continued. "So we went back to fishing. As fast he we caught the sunfish, we flipped them out on the bank. That 'coon stayed with us half an hour, eating fresh fish 'til he was so full he could hold no more. Then he looked at us for a minute with as big a 'thank you' as you ever saw—and ambled off into the bushes."

Often, unfortunately, the wild creature is betrayed in his trust. The spruce grouse of the evergreen forests of my own northern New England and Canada is sometimes called "fool hen" because it permits man to come up to it and hit it with a stick. And "dumb as a Dodo" shows what man himself thinks of the huge flightless bird that let itself be approached closely enough to be slaughtered. Yet the bond between humans and wild animals continues to exist.

Perhaps it was this bond that led the first wolf-dogs to share primitive man's hearth. Perhaps this bond led a buck deer to wander through the streets of my town a few years ago, allowing people to pet him.

Alan Devoe speaks of this same attraction in *Our Animal Neighbors,* when he tells of surprising a sleeping fox in a snowbank:

. . . The fox stood looking at me alertly, but he made no move to run away. This was very odd. Foxes are the wariest of our animal neighbors, and any animal startled from sleep assumes danger. Probably, I thought, the fox had not yet "placed" me as a human being, for from the first instant of his tumultuous breakout from his sleeping place I had stood perfectly motionless, just another snow-flecked silent object in a world of white silence.

But then, as fox and I regarded each other steadily, it seemed

161

to me that he was staring so fixedly and sniffing the icy air so carefully from such a very little distance away, that he could not possibly be missing the truth about me. It was as though there were a kind of spell between us.

When some minutes had passed—really only some seconds, I suppose—I broke the spell. I reached out and snapped off a stick of dead hemlock. It made a *crack*! like a gunshot in the frosty stillness. Considerably hampered by my heavy jacket, I drew back my arm and shied the hemlock stick at the fox.

The stick dropped into the fluffy snow several feet short of him.

It seemed to me it had scarcely landed when the fox plunged forward toward me in great springing leaps, pounced on the stick, grabbed it, and whirled away. With the ducking, weaving prance of a triumphant collie, he bounded off through the snow, his treasure gripped in his narrow jaws. He ran as hard as he could go now, trotting, jumping, floundering, and struggling through the white depths. In a moment or two he had vanished among far snow-bowed evergreens. I was alone in the winter silence.

However much a naturalist loves his animal neighbors, he dislikes false sentimentality about them. But I don't believe I have to be ashamed to say that as I stood, still motionless with astonishment in the bitter woods, I felt a certain pricking in my eyes not altogether from the cold. No one, as I said a while ago, seems to have whistled to *Vulpes fulva* back in the dawn of things. No one threw him a stick. But there is a part of him—just shown me on a winter morning, as a secret might be trusted to a friend —that for all the millenniums of lonely wildness has perhaps been ready and waiting. . . .

It's this possibility of the unexpected, this potential of discovery, that adds so much to our life in the country. We can never tell when something new may happen.

Just as I wrote these words, our bridge rumbled with the weight

162

of an automobile passing over it. Perhaps our approaching visitor made the telephone call I received earlier about a wild rabbit with a broken leg.

Perhaps Peg had better get a few old lettuce leaves from the storekeeper. Just in case.

CHAPTER FOURTEEN

With a Few
Simple Things . . .

NOT LONG AGO I was telling a friend of the fun we have in learning about the animals and plants that share this land with us.

"But you've got an advantage," he protested. "You live right in the country where it's easy to see all those things.

"Look at me, though. I live in the middle of town. I can't just peek out the back door and see a bluebird. And my apartment doesn't have a back door—except the fire escape."

Undeniably I did have a head start. I can remember few days in my life when I haven't been in contact with the outdoors in some way or other. Yet even a confirmed urbanite can enjoy the pursuit of plants and animals in their own surroundings. It's mainly for his benefit that I offer the following random suggestions for enriching both his everyday life and his vacation away from the city.

THERE ARE few cities with no parks or natural areas somewhere within their boundaries. Often these are fertile fields to study, for they may have been planted to a number of species of trees and shrubs in addition to the native kinds. Even in Central Park, right in Manhattan, you can find many different birds, plus assorted insects, a snake or two, and a number of frogs.

Actually, this is where I heard my first spring peeper last year.

WITH A FEW SIMPLE THINGS...

I happened to be walking through the park one late February day when I heard the brave piping note of the tiny frog above the distant clamor of the big city. I could have been in a Maine marsh or a Pennsylvania swamp, but I wasn't. I was in New York City. And I've seen nighthawks, those erratic flyers with the white wing-patches, scooping insects from the air above the heart of Detroit on a summer night.

The truth is that animals and plants are ever seeking to expand their range. Once the opossum, the praying mantis and the cardinal were all creatures of the South; now they're found well up into my own state of Vermont. And the evening grosbeak, which used to be considered a bird of the North, is now a common winter visitor well below New York City. Very few possibilities are unexplored by wild creatures.

One of my students collected fifty-one separate species of insects from the classroom windows during the school year. Another did spare-time birdwatching with a pair of binoculars from the Biology laboratory and came up with a score of forty species in the shrubbery outside.

Thus anyone can take advantage of this tendency of living things to spread beyond their normal habitat.

Attracting birds is possible even in the heart of a city, as I've mentioned earlier.

Of course the variety will be limited, but even pigeons and starlings can be wonderful teachers in the ways of wild things. In fact, I have read somewhere that in certain parts of the world starlings are caught and confined as cage-birds. And well they might be, for their repertoire of whistles and imitations is amazing. They can produce the liquid warble of a bluebird or the harsh cry of a jay with such perfection that you look for the two blue-coated birds in the tree and find only a glossy black starling.

If you live where there is any vegetation near by at all, you should be able to attract at least the common birds of the region.

A feeding tray is helpful, but not necessary. In fact, there will be some birds slow to use a feeder unless it's only a foot or two above the ground. These are the ones which normally feed on the ground—such as juncos, tree sparrows and snow buntings.

If you use a tray, though, its elegance makes little difference to the birds that come to it. The best tray—whether it's an old milk carton or a glassed-in gadget that is pivoted to swing away from the wind—is one which allows the birds good visibility and provides easy access and exit.

Food should never be lacking for long, as the birds come to depend on this supply. I recall one time being desperate for birdfood, so I placed the shells from a bowl of mixed nuts on the feeder. Nuthatches, chickadees and sparrows all had a feast, gleaning pieces I hadn't found with the nutpick.

Grapefruit rinds and leftover cereal will serve in a pinch, too. But beware of uncooked wheat grains in too great quantity: sparrows and juncos will eat them whole, and the grain will swell in the birds' crops, causing misery or death.

Babysitting a young animal or an orphaned bird will prompt this question first: "What do I feed it?"

This is likely to be a problem, but not an insurmountable one. There are a few basic foods found around most homes that will be acceptable emergency rations until you can experiment and work out your own formula.

For young animals which are not yet weaned, milk and honey make a fine food. Cow's milk is usually quite rich, so I add about two tablespoons of warm water to a cup of milk. A tablespoon of honey per cup of milk mixture adds to its palatability. Sometimes a dash of salt in the formula will help.

Medicine droppers are better than doll bottles, but be sure you don't force the food down so it gags the little throat. Sometimes a cotton swab wet with formula can be placed on the lips and mouth of the baby animal; this may start him to licking his lips even though he wouldn't take a bottle or medicine dropper.

It's far better to feed often—every three or four hours—and in small amounts, rather than two or three times a day in quantity.

Babyfoods of all kinds make good rations for slightly older birds and animals.

Adult animals can be fed various raw vegetables if they're vegetarians (such as rabbits).

Those with more general food habits (such as mice, rats and chipmunks) can be given a combined raisin/peanut butter/rolled oat/bacon mix.

Canned dogfood is fine for the meat-eaters. It's clean and easily obtained. Bits of liver and hamburger make fine food, but do not get too much fat in the 'burger.

Also, in all feeding be sure to get rid of leftovers quickly before they begin to spoil in the nest.

Frogs, salamanders, many fish and reptiles prefer moving prey.

I often put a piece of liver on the tip of a slender broomstraw and jiggle it in front of a frog or salamander. They'll attack it readily, while the same piece of liver lying inertly in their dish would be completely ignored. I've seen frogs by the edge of a stream jump at a blowing leaf just because it was moving.

Or try the tip of the tail of an earthworm, which, when severed from the body, wriggles in convincing fashion. (This apparently does little harm to the worm: it merely grows a new tail.)

Note that if you find you must keep a wild animal more than a day or so, it's best to check with the authorities. Here in Vermont we can let animals roam around the yard with freedom to come and go as they please, as long as they're not confined in any way. Then they find their way back to the wild in their own good time.

This was the case of a cottontail rabbit our son Tom brought home two years ago. It had been mauled by dogs. After we'd tended its wounds and fed it for a day or so, we let it go in our

167

back yard. It remained for two or three days longer and finally disappeared. We still see it occasionally at dusk, however, easily identifiable by one tattered ear.

MUCH OF our "collecting" of plants and animals has been done miles away from our hundred Vermont acres. We have lain on our stomachs and watched the bison of Wichita Mountains Wildlife Refuge in Oklahoma through binoculars, and scanned the kelp beds of the California coast in a vain search for the rare sea otter. We've walked out into the Arizona desert with the only other visible living creature a turkey vulture circling hopefully above our heads. We've marveled at Old Faithful as it "played" right on schedule at Yellowstone, and stood humbled before the incomparable jewel of my favorite of all parks—Crater Lake's incredibly blue waters.

Of course we'll never get to know an elk as well as we know our own eastern whitetail deer, nor will a desert tortoise ever seem as familiar as our own Vermont wood turtle, but the comparison helps in our knowledge of both.

The cost of such trips in our inexpensive micro-bus is small.

On three separate trips where we kept close tabs on every penny —one to Florida, another to Chincoteague, and a third on a grand tour which covered thirty states from coast to coast—we discovered that these trips cost the six of us only three dollars more a day per person than it would have cost to stay at home.

Eighteen dollars a day, in other words, total cost of gas, oil, lodging and the few souvenirs we bought. We figure we'd have to eat anyway, even if we were at home, so we don't count food.

Most of our souvenirs are things like a tiny cone from a sequoia tree, an abalone shell from a California beach, or a bit of red soil from Carolina. To us these mean more than manmade mementos, mass-produced somewhere and then lettered with the appropriate name of the area where they are to be displayed.

168

Our tent and sleeping bags nearly eliminate the cost of lodging. Very few tentsites cost more than five dollars a night (total cost per campsite), while National Forest sites are often free. National Parks may have a concession or charges amounting to a dollar or two per person for tenting.

Everyone travels according to his own rules, of course. We may go three hundred miles (seldom, if ever, farther)in a day, and not move at all the next day. We often avoid the superhighways: they're fine for travel, but you don't really see the land. The better campsites are so popular that we try to arrive by midafternoon. Few things can spoil your fun more than arriving late, hungry and tired —and then to find that all the sites are taken.

Note: don't be in a hurry to leave the car if you happen to spot an animal or bird from your automobile.

Many wild creatures will allow an auto to approach closely, whereas a person sneaking along would be regarded with immediate suspicion. So keep in the car and drive up slowly. You may be surprised at how close you can get.

Ice cubes make wonderful pacifiers—for adults and children alike.

We've discovered on our trips that they're easily found nearly anywhere in the United States at dispensers outside gas stations and supermarkets. We recommend them for three reasons: they're something to chew on, they satisfy thirst, and they're a cold treat on a summer day.

We keep them in a clean insulated container. They melt slowly all day, and by suppertime there is icewater for punch as well.

Automobile associations, such as the AAA and ALA, list campgrounds and facilities as well as hotels and motels. They will provide a detailed map of the route for members, and are a wonderful help if your car develops trouble.

Most major oil companies can also route you to your destination.

You can also write for specific information to the park or forest which you plan to visit.

Specimens are often desirable even with my type of collecting, in which the animal or plant is left undisturbed.

Ordinary isopropyl rubbing alcohol makes a serviceable "pickle" for animal and insect specimens.

A jar to put insects to sleep painlessly can be made from a pint mayonnaise jar. Moisten a wad of paper toweling and place it in the bottom of the jar, where it will soon release its lethal fumes. Place a few discs of cardboard on top of the moist paper so the insects will not touch it, because it sometimes affects their natural color. Carbon tetrachloride can be used as the killing fluid.

Plants can't be kept satisfactorily in most preservatives, as they lose their color. They are best placed between sheets of newspaper.

Take care to get a plant which has blossoms, if possible. Spread it on the paper so the blossoms are displayed to their fullest, holding it in place with tabs of wet paper of necessary. Put a second piece of newspaper on top, and press the plant between blotters under several heavy books or a piece of board. Do not disturb it for two weeks or more.

In all cases, be sure you make a note as to where the specimen was found, time of year, and type of situation (grassy field, forest, etc.). These notes are often valuable clues in identification later on.

Plastic bags make good containers for all sorts of things. They fold into a tiny square which is easily carried in the pocket. They're fine to keep plant specimens moist on the way back to camp. They make good emergency rainhats and camera covers in a downpour.

Field guides add to the enjoyment of such trips. Among them are the celebrated *Field Guide to the Birds* by Roger Tory Peterson, and his companion volume, *Field Guide to Western Birds;* both are part of the series published by Houghton Mifflin Company. You can get a field guide for almost anything—plant, animal, or mineral.

WITH A FEW SIMPLE THINGS...

The late Henry Hill Collins, Jr., wrote the *Complete Field Guide to American Wildlife* (published by Harper and Brothers), which is a handy one-volume work to identify almost any creature but the spiders and insects of east, central and northern North America.

G. P. Putnam's Sons publishes a group of Nature Field Books, several of which I carry in my knapsack.

With binoculars, high power does not necessarily mean the best instrument. Motions of the hand and body are magnified, too, as the image is magnified.

I find a 6 x 30 or a 7 x 35 binocular best for general tramping. Lean against a tree or sit down for steadiest vision when using them.

Some types focus with a center knob, while in others each eyepiece focuses individually. The one you prefer is a matter of individual taste. Both have their good points.

Cameras, of course, are a complete subject in themselves. I claim little authority as to which one may be best. As with binoculars, there's a wide variety in individual taste. Some of the best pictures in my files were taken with a simple point-and-shoot camera. But whatever camera you use, be sure to keep extra film on hand. And don't hesitate to get variety in your shots.

Shoot into the general direction of the sun for silhouettes and back-lighted pictures.

Take pictures through windows—provided there'll be no reflection from the glass or from a flashbulb. I've seen people creak a window open to get a picture of an animal or bird just outside—with the result that the stealthy opening of the sash scared the subject away. The picture of the ermine that's included in this book was one I took through glass.

As a photographer told me some time ago: "The best picture in the world, with the most perfect light, the most interesting subject and the finest camera is no good—unless you take it."

In much of the work for my illustrated nature talks I use a Minolta SRT-101, with telephoto lenses for special work. As I sit at my typewriter in my upstairs study, the Minolta is pointed out the window with a 400-mm telephoto lens attached, ready to "collect" a bluebird which is thinking about taking up residence in a birdhouse I erected a few days ago.

So IF you'd sample your portion of the rich heritage still left to us in our cities or countryside, first take along all your senses and your imagination, and then pack your camera and plastic bags and binoculars and field books. Or if you're interested and receptive, you'll find that your wild neighbors will often come to you. No matter how you go about it, though, there's something new waiting for you.

And who knows? Maybe you can have a loon in your bathtub, too.

INDEX

Adaptation, 121
Alcohol, 48, 92
Algae, 27
Amoeba, 29
Animals, adult, care, 167
Animals, young, care, 166-167
Ants, 114-115, 121
  army, 114
  guests (inquilines), 114-115
  nest, artificial, 114
Aphids, 77
Arrowheads, 31-32
Assateague Island, 140-143
Autotomy, 45

Back-swimmer, 25
Barnacles, 43-44, 46
Bathtub, animal storage, 82-90, 92
Bears, 158-159
Beavers, 48
Bees, 46, 160
  bumblebee, 46
Beetle, 46, 92, 115, 116, 153
  dung, 115, 116
  grub, 92
  Japanese, 46
Behavior, acquired, 121
Behavior, animal, 111-122
Birch, 99, 155
  river, 99
Birds, 100, 101-110, 165-167
  attracting, 165, 166
  feeding, 101-110
  territory in, 104
  young, 100, 104-105, 166-167
Binoculars, 168, 171

Blackbirds, 20, 30
Blackflies, 48-49, 92
Black widow, *see* Spider
Blaisdell, Harold, 160-161
Blowfly, 98
Bluebird, 109, 164, 165
Bluefish, 49, 50
Bobcat, 19
Bunting, snow, 166
Burgess, Thornton, 2, 29

Cameras, 171-172
Campgrounds, 169-170
"Camp robber," *see* Jay, Canada
Carbon tetrachloride, 170
Cardinal, 165
Catbird, 100, 102, 104
Caterpillar, 3, 100, 116
  tent, 3-5
Catfish, 86
Centipede, 31
Cherry, 3, 155
Chickadee, 104, 105, 106, 112, 166
Chincoteague Island, 139-149
Chipmunk, 14, 68, 95, 104, 112
Ciliates, 29
Cladocera, 28
Crater Lake, 107-108, 168
Cockroaches, 43
Collins, Henry Hill, Jr., 171
Crab, 28, 43, 45, 46, 61
  ghost, 43-46, 61
    autotomy, 45
Cricket, 29
Crow, 15-18, 154
Cyanide, 47

Dead Creek Wildlife Refuge, 95
Deer, 19, 25-26, 27, 91, 99-100, 152,
    157, 161, 168
  fawn, 19, 25-26, 99
Dennis, Wesley, 141
Devoe, Alan, 161-162
Dove, mourning, 95
Dragonfly, 20, 46
Ducks, 7, 86, 96-97
  incubation of, 96-97
  Muscovy, 7-9
  scaup, 86
  wild, 7-8

Earthworms, 137
Elm, 62-63
Ermine, 153

Field guides, 170-171
Fish, 85, 121, 161, 167, 185
  behavior, 121
  killifish, 185
  sunfish, 161
Flea, 46-47
Flicker, 104
Flies, 47-49, 92, 153
  black, 48-49, 92
  bot, 47
  crane, 153
  horse, 47-48
Flycatcher, 99
"Fool hen," see Grouse, spruce
Formaldehyde, 45
Fox, 81, 154, 157, 161-162
  red, 154, 157, 161-162
Frog, 5-7, 20, 21, 27, 28, 29, 62, 74,
    82, 86, 89, 90, 164, 167
  bullfrog, 86
  color change in, 90
  eggs, 75
  green, 21
  peeper, spring, 29, 164-165

Galls, insect, 63
Grasshopper, 29, 43, 116-117
Grosbeak, evening, 165
Grouse, spruce, 161
Gulls, 154

Hawk, 31, 95, 109, 112

Cooper's, 109, 112
Hemlock, 2
Henry, Marguerite, 141
Hornet, 113
Horses, 47-48, 49, 139-149
Horsetail, see Rush, scouring
Hydra, 28

Inquilines, 114-115
Insectivores, 24
Instinct, 116-121

Jack-in-the-pulpit, 157
Jay, 103, 106-109, 154, 165
  blue, 103, 106, 107, 109, 165
  Canada, 108
  intelligence, 107-108
Jellyfish, 43, 46, 49, 50, 61
Junco, 166

Killifish, 85
Kingfisher, 91

Leaf miners, 63
Lice, 46
Lichens, 31
Lily, calla, 157
Lizards, 45
Lobster, 28
Loon, 82-86, 159
  food of, 85

Mantis, praying, 165
Maple, 155
Merganser, 86
Microscope, homemade, 28-29
Mint, 156
Misty of Chincoteague, 141
Mites, 16-17, 28
Molluscs, 43
Mosquitoes, 28, 43
Moth, 153
Mouse, 23, 72, 93-94, 111-112, 121,
    152-153, 160
  jumping, 152-153
Mud-dauber, see Wasp
Muskrat, 20, 21, 27, 29, 86-89, 92,
  157

Nest, hornet, 92
Nighthawk, 165

INDEX

Nutcracker, Clark's, 108
Nuthatch, 102, 106, 166

Opossum, 165
Oriole, 102, 104
Owl, 70-74, 156
  barn, 70-74

Parasites, 48
Peach, 155
Peterson, Roger Tory, 170
Pigeon, 119, 154, 165
Pine, 2
Planarian, 28
Pony, Chincoteague, 139-149
Porcupine, 159-160
Preservatives, 45, 50, 170
Procyon lotor, see Raccoon

Rabbit, 81, 163, 167-168
  cottontail, 81
Raccoon, 20, 32-42, 97-99, 160-161
  food habits, 38
  young, feeding of, 98-99
Radioactivity, 135-136
Rat, 14, 72-73
Redwing, *see* Blackbird
Refrigerator, animals in, 89-90
Reptiles, 167
Robin, 3, 102, 104
Rush, scouring, 155-156

Salamander, 27, 62, 89, 153, 167
Sassafras, 155
Sea lion, 90
Sedge, 156
Senses, use of, 155-156
Shenandoah Nat'l. Park, 149
Shrew, 23-24
  masked, 23
  water, 23-24
Skunk, 92, 156-158
Skunk cabbage, 157
Skyline Drive, Va., 148
Snails, 43
Snakes, 7, 11-14, 21, 95, 136-137, 164
  black, 13-14, 95
  garter, 11-13, 136-137
  ribbon, 21
Sparrow, 31, 94, 102, 103, 106, 108,
    109, 119, 166
  English, 103, 106
  song, 31, 102, 108, 109
  tree, 106, 166
Spider, 24, 31, 46, 76-81, 92-95, 116,
    117, 121, 153
  black widow, 46, 76-81, 94
  tarantula, 92-95
  water, 24
Swallow, barn, 17
Springtail (insects), 31
Spruce, 155
Squirrel, 68, 103, 108, 119, 121, 160
  gray, 119
  ground, 68, 108
Starfish, 50
Starling, 119, 165
Sumac, 155
Sunfish, 161

Tackapausha Park, 62, 85-86
Tanager, scarlet, 102
Tapeworm, 28, 46
Tarantula, *see* Spider
Teaching, rewards of, 134-138
Tests, biology, 131-134
Thrush, 156
Tide, variation in, 51-52
Toad, 15, 119-121
  feeding habits, 120
  longevity, 15
Tom-Bill bug, *see* Beetle, dung
Travel, cost of, 168-169
Trophallaxis, 114, 121
Tumblebug, *see* Beetle, dung
Turtle, 2, 7, 14, 19, 21, 25, 27, 29,
    82, 86, 90, 95, 168
  diamondback terrapin, 86
  painted, 19, 27
  snapping, 86
  spotted, 14, 21, 25
  wood, 14, 90, 95
Tyto alba, see Owl, barn

Urchins, sea, 50-52

Veery, 98
Vorticella, 29
Vulpes fulva, see Fox, red

Warbler, yellow, 108-109
Wasp, 113, 114, 116-119
  digger, 116-117
  drone (male), 113
  food of, 113-114
  grubs, 113-114
  mud-dauber, 117-119
  trophallaxis in, 113-114
Water boatman, 24
Weasel, 153
"Whiskey Jack," see Jay, Canada
Wichita Mountains Nat'l. Wildlife
  Refuge, 115, 168

"Wild brother," 157
Wildcat, see Bobcat
Woodchuck, 64-69, 154-155
  food habits, 69
  hibernation, 65, 68
  teeth of, 66
Woodpecker, 101, 103-104, 109-110
  downy, 103-104
  hairy, 101, 109-110
Woods lore, 152-157

Yellowstone Nat'l. Park, 158-159, 168

CHRISTIAN HERALD ASSOCIATION AND ITS MINISTRIES

CHRISTIAN HERALD ASSOCIATION, founded in 1878, publishes The Christian Herald Magazine, one of the leading interdenominational religious monthlies in America. Through its wide circulation, it brings inspiring articles and the latest news of religious developments to many families. From the magazine's pages came the initiative for CHRISTIAN HERALD CHILDREN and THE BOWERY MISSION, two individually supported not-for-profit corporations.

CHRISTIAN HERALD CHILDREN, established in 1894, is the name for a unique and dynamic ministry to disadvantaged children, offering hope and opportunities which would not otherwise be available for reasons of poverty and neglect. The goal is to develop each child's potential and to demonstrate Christian compassion and understanding to children in need.

Mont Lawn is a permanent camp located in Bushkill, Pennsylvania. It is the focal point of a ministry which provides a healthful "vacation with a purpose" to children who without it would be confined to the streets of the city. Up to 1000 children between the age of 7 and 11 come to Mont Lawn each year.

Christian Herald Children maintains year-round contact with children by means of a *City Youth Ministry.* Central to its philosophy is the belief that only through sustained relationships and demonstrated concern can individual lives be truly enriched. Special emphasis is on individual guidance, spiritual and family counseling and tutoring. This follow-up ministry to inner-city children culminates for many in financial assistance toward higher education and career counseling.

THE BOWERY MISSION, located at 227 Bowery, New York City, has since 1879 been reaching out to the lost men on the Bowery, offering them what could be their last chance to rebuild their lives. Every man is fed, clothed and ministered to. Countless numbers have entered the 90-day residential rehabilitation program at the Bowery Mission. A concentrated ministry of counseling, medical care, nutrition therapy, Bible study and Gospel services awakens a man to spiritual renewal within himself.

These ministries are supported solely by the voluntary contributions of individuals and by legacies and bequests. Contributions are tax deductible. Checks should be made out either to CHRISTIAN HERALD CHILDREN or to THE BOWERY MISSION.

Administrative Office: 40 Overlook Drive, Chappaqua, New York 10514
Telephone: (914) 769-9000